In an age of gender-correctness gon
struggling with confusion and delaye
refreshing word to males everywhere.
that, here's how. A male you care about needs this excellent book.

—MARK RUTLAND,
FOUNDER, NATIONAL INSTITUTE OF CHRISTIAN LEADERSHIP,
FORMER COLLEGE PRESIDENT,
NEW YORK TIMES BEST-SELLING AUTHOR

The Rev. Dr. Clarence Boyd has written *Endangered Masculinity* to address
a very serious problem in contemporary society. The book comes out of his
deep concern about the spiritual and cultural erosion of manhood, partic-
ularly in America. The biblical concept of manhood has taken a serious
beating in America, especially through the images of men portrayed in the
media. The social and cultural climate created by the baby boomers and the
architects of the sexual revolution of the 1960s have created a distorted view
of manhood that has been normalized by the media. As a new generation
of men and women take this view as normative, this distortion has significant and serious consequences for America and her families. Based on his
experience as a minister of the gospel and Dean of Spiritual Formation at
a mission-driven Christian university, Boyd addresses the issue of masculinity in a theological, practical, and thought-provoking way. He sees man as
God's creation, made in His own image. He sees woman and family hidden
in the original man. He recognizes the equality of men and women before
God and the power of God's anointing on all. He deals with leadership,
relationship, and the power of God's purpose and anointing. Regardless of
the readers' theological perspectives, this book is sure to generate a much-
needed conversation about men, women, masculinity, and family. May
God's purpose for this volume be accomplished!

—THOMSON K. MATHEW, D. MIN., ED. D.,
DEAN, COLLEGE OF THEOLOGY AND MINISTRY
ORAL ROBERTS UNIVERSITY

Boyd's *Endangered Masculinity* reaffirmed to me the long reach of God's arms in our lives—always reminding us of His perfect picture for our human journey. Into the shattered circumstances many may face, His love still stands at the door, watching and waiting for our return. I was personally challenged to fully and joyfully embrace my transforming responsibilities within my home and beyond my doors.

—CLIFTON L. TAULBERT
AUTHOR, *ONCE UPON A TIME WHEN WE WERE COLORED*
AND *EIGHT HABITS OF THE HEART*

The foundation of family, government, and the world is horribly fractured. Every man who is in a position of leadership or influence feels the weight of these foundational stress fractures. As men, we do everything within our power to shore up the foundation that is crumbling beneath our feet. Yet with all of our innovative programs of human design, we fall very short in our goal to heal broken foundations that lead to poverty, lack of education, war, famine and disease. Men, we are standing on shaking ground, and our so-called wise decisions are like shifting sands. Could it be that we are missing the point of living lives of purpose? Are we losing the precious gift of manhood? In his book *Endangered Masculinity*, Dr. Clarence Boyd confronts and challenges every man to examine his life and find where he is lacking. *Endangered Masculinity* examines how, as men, we are busy in our pursuit of happiness but neglecting the essential elements of faith, hope, and love which enable us to live a life of purpose. If man is right with God, then man is right with his family, his government, and the world. And that's a sure foundation upon which a kingdom can stand.

—KELLY WRIGHT
TV NEWS ANCHOR, FOX NEWS

I am confident that this book will resonate enormously with men and women regardless of age and position in life. Tackling a topic that addresses issues like the decline of masculinity at its spiritual root can be dangerous because most fear taking a position on the issues addressed in this book. Thank God Dr. Boyd has been given the insight into the spiritual battles that must be fought to win this battle and the courage to address head-on the topic of the erosion of manhood that is affecting homes across this nation and around the world.

—HAMISH C. REED
CEO, BRANCHES MEDICAL INC.

Over the last twenty-five years I've watched Clarence Boyd lead hundreds of young men into greatness. Now he shares his wisdom and tools for equipping a generation into God's path of identity and greatness from childhood to manhood.

—LYNETTE LEWIS
AUTHOR, SPEAKER, BUSINESS CONSULTANT

I am so excited about Dr. Boyd's new book *Endangered Masculinity*. In a world where many are raised without a godly father figure in their lives, it can be hard to know what it truly means to live life as a man of God, but Dr. Boyd knows.

As the Dean of Students at Oral Roberts University for years, Dr. Boyd has studied and shown what it means to live life as a man set on God's best. Throughout the years, he poured that knowledge into many lives, including my own. I'm so grateful for the life he has lived and for the wisdom that he shares. I am confident that this book will inspire you to become the man God has called you to be!

—JIM GRAFF
LEAD PASTOR, FAITH FAMILY CHURCH
FOUNDER, THE SIGNIFICANT CHURCH NETWORK

endangered
masculinity

Foreword by Dr. Myles Munroe

endangered
masculinity

The Spiritual and Cultural
Erosion of Manhood

Dr. Clarence V. Boyd, Jr.

HONOR✛NET
PUBLISHERS

SAPULPA, OK

Endangered Masculinity: The Spiritual and Cultural Erosion of Manhood

ISBN: 978-1-938021-21-3

Copyright © 2014 by Clarence V. Boyd

Clarence Boyd, Jr.
P. O. Box 48642
Tulsa, OK 74148

Unless otherwise indicated, all Scripture quotations are taken from the Holy Bible, New International Version. Copyright © 1973, 1978, 1984, International Bible Society. Used by permission.

Scripture quotations marked GNT are from the Good News Translation of the Bible. Copyright © 1992 American Bible Society.

Scripture quotations marked KJV are from the King James Version of the Bible.

Scripture quotations marked NKJV are from the New King James Version of the Bible. Copyright © 1979, 1980, 1982 by Thomas Nelson, Inc., publishers. Used by permission.

Published by HonorNet
PO Box 910
Sapulpa, OK 74067
honornet.net

Cover by boydcoalescence.com

I dedicate this book

To the revelation that in every man there is a king.
It would be a shame to live your life and never reign, and
Though your kingship will always be challenged,
Never settle for the man and miss the king.

To the mandate that every man must know his Heavenly Father,
Know his identity, Know his purpose, and
Know his measure of rule and his sphere of influence.

To the calling of every man to his home and family,
To his workplace and his community, and
To the Kingdom of God and His Church.

To my RRTM family,
My RRTEC family,
My ORU family,
and

To my wife who is my best friend,
To my children who remain my inspiration,
To my parents who are my examples, and
To my siblings who help me appreciate family…

May God be Glorified.

ACKNOWLEDGMENTS

acknowledge my Heavenly Father who hides in me His revelation for the male-man and the mandate that He restore order to all under His covering. May each man become the spiritual king of his home and family.

I must thank Dr. Myles Munroe, my spiritual father and mentor, who saw in me what I did not see in myself. It was his consistent inspiration that allowed me to see what the Father had deposited in me. May he and his wife Ruth know that they are God-ordained examples for men and families everywhere.

To my wife, Dr. Kim Boyd, who stands by my side believing in me and encouraging me to become all that God created me to be. To my children and their families who provide the focus, discipline, and vision necessary to accomplish this work. I also want to acknowledge Ms. Pearl Tracey, Mrs. Melanie Gross, and Mr. Hamish Reed, who literally walked with me through this process and helped me believe that this was God's will for my life.

Finally, I acknowledge every mother, wife, sister, and daughter who yearns for a king in her life. May the man in your life realize that inside of him lies a king, and may he provide each of you with the covering you so rightly deserve. May every man in your life become the king he was created to be!

CONTENTS

FOREWORD

ndangered Masculinity, The Spiritual and Cultural Erosion of Manhood is an erudite, eloquent, and immensely thought-provoking work that gets to the heart of the deepest passions and aspirations of the heart of all men—to discover what is true manhood and how one can achieve it.

Endangered Masculinity is indispensable reading for anyone who wants to understand what a real man is and the qualities of true manhood and the value they bring to the community. This is a profound authoritative work that spans the wisdom of the ages and yet breaks new ground in its approach to understanding the modern man. This book will possibly become a classic in this and the next generation.

This exceptional work by Dr. Boyd is one of the most profound, practical, principle-centered approaches to the subject of true manhood I have read in a long time. The author's approach to this timely issue brings a fresh breath of air that captivates the heart, engages the mind, and inspires the spirit of the reader.

The title of this book alone, *Endangered Masculinity: The Spiritual and Cultural Erosion of Manhood,* should make it a must-read not only for all men, but also for any woman who has a father, brother, son, or husband in her life. Culture and the erosion of what a true Godly man looks and acts like have left this current generation feeling fatherless. It is the biggest issue facing us, both in the church and world. Without role models and guidance, how are our young men going to find their way? God created man to lead, and it is the number one diabolical scheme of the enemy to crumble nations, families, churches and homes...—to remove the man.

There is not a race, culture, or group of people on the planet who are not being devastated by this attack on man and his identity. It is a continuation of the Garden of Eden when the serpent deceived man concerning what was good and evil. *Endangered Masculinity* is a clarion cry to all nations, cultures, and races to heed the call to stand up for Godly manhood before it is extinct. I have known Dr. Boyd for many years, and the wisdom he has gained over the years fighting on the front lines for young men is reflected in this book.

The author's ability to leap over complicated theological and metaphysical jargon and reduce complex theories to simple practical principles that the least among us can understand is amazing.

This work will challenge the intellectual while embracing the layman as it dismantles the mysteries of the soul search of mankind and delivers the profound with simplicity.

Dr. Boyd's approach awakens in the reader the untapped inhibitors that retard our personal development as men. And his antidotes empower us to rise above these self-defeating, self-limiting factors to a life of exploits in spiritual and mental advancement. Every man and his sons must read this book.

The author also integrates into each chapter the time-tested precepts that give each principle a practical application to life making the entire process people-friendly.

Endangered Masculinity is pregnant with wisdom and powerful principles, and I enjoyed the mind-expanding experience of this exciting work. I admonish you to plunge into this ocean of knowledge and watch your life change for the better as a twenty-first century man.

—Dr. Myles Munroe
Best-selling author, pastor, leadership mentor, and founder
of Bahamas Faith Ministry International, Nassau, Bahamas

PREFACE

I t is amazing today that the very concept of manhood is being challenged while the perception of fatherhood has been taken for granted. In other words, men have lost sight of man's original purpose, and the concept of manhood has become vague. In similar fashion, a new generation of the male human has arrived with little or no realization of what manhood truly involves. Somehow this new generation has been birthed with little revelation of boundaries and standards that distinguish them as men or qualify them as fathers. Regardless of the time passed or the ground lost, men must again be introduced to their measure of rule and their sphere of influence. Every man must realize that manhood is not a title and fatherhood is not an achievement.

Manhood is defined as (a) the condition of being a human being; (b) qualities associated with men: manliness; and (c) the condition of being an adult male as distinguished from a child or female. In a general sense, manhood may represent humanity. This makes sense when one realizes that man was created both male and female and given the awesome responsibility of dominion. However, the responsibility of dominion must always be understood in the correct context. If dominion is taken out of its original context, the result will always be abuse. Man will assume that he has rulership of all things. When man fails to exercise authority over those things he was created to rule, he has abused his own role of leadership by not leading. He will experience frustration by attempting to control things he was never given authority over.

Manhood must also be understood from a position of distinctiveness. Put another way, some things cannot represent manhood because they are not a reflection of what manhood was originally created to be. A man cannot assume he is mature just because he is a male. Everything male is not necessarily a man. The majority of you reading this book have potentially experienced this reality. You more than likely know someone who is a man chronologically, yet a child when it comes to being responsible as a leader, a husband, or a provider. Manhood is a complicated reality but must be understood in its proper context. Men can only comprehend their identities and purposes from their Creator. When men operate in their purposes, their identities are secure. However, when men abandon their created purposes, their identities are compromised. When men experience this challenge, the result will always be a forfeiture of their original purposes. As a result, a man must change his identity in order to accommodate his newfound purpose.

Society today promotes the redefining of manhood. A generation of young men are witnessing this attack upon their purposes without any revelation of its effects upon them. Is it any wonder that today's generation of young men are more confused about their identities than previous generations before them? According to *The Merriam-Webster Dictionary*, the definition of manhood includes a distinction between what is male as opposed to what is female. In this sense manhood can be understood by its comparison to what it is not. In the same way that childhood characteristics do not represent true manhood, it must be understood that any confusion about the identity of manhood being compromised with female or feminine characteristics will also have detrimental consequences when it comes to men living out their divine purposes. Men will never be able to comprehend their purposes if they are blinded to the original purpose for man. Once blinded to his purpose, a man will adapt his identity to his newly perceived purpose. This reality is evident in our society today as we witness the absence of men in the home as well as the subtle attack of the enemy upon manhood itself. If the purpose for a man is redefined, serious consideration must be given to the impact this change will have on his perception of his own identity.

This book seeks to address the need to return to the original purpose for which man was created. His identity and purpose must once again be understood in its correct context. Too many men have already been lost, a new generation of young men struggle with compromised definitions of manhood, and the consequences of this confusion continue to have staggering effects on the family, our communities at large, and life as it was meant to be.

INTRODUCTION

The word *cover* has many meanings. In its simplest form, it means to "place something over or upon, as for protection, concealment, or warmth." This implies that those who are covered need covering from others whose motive is to harm them. It also implies that one may need covering in order to have his or her needs met. In either case, covering is important. From a biblical perspective, the word *cover* is synonymous with the word *veil*, which implies something that is spread out for the purpose of covering. To cover could mean to cover up or over. It also could mean to cover around or to cover together. The point is that covering speaks to the responsibility to provide for those being covered while protecting those covered from external forces that would harm them.

Man, the male man, is constantly searching for his purpose. What does this purpose look like? This is one of the greatest needs that man has. The man must come to grips with his purpose if he is to fulfill it. In other words, a man's search for his purpose is also his quest for his manhood. When a man discovers his purpose, he also realizes his manhood. The two are intimately attached. Any man confused about his purpose will also struggle with his identity and how to fulfill or represent authentic manhood. Society wants a man to think that he is still a man in spite of the fact that he may not represent authentic manhood. A man's purpose and identity come from his Creator, and apart from this reality, every man will seek blindly after his purpose and question his own manhood.

God created everything to be covered. This is a living principle that must be respected and practiced in one's everyday life. No one was created to be without covering. In fact when men or women find themselves without covering, they quickly realize that they are vulnerable and exposed to external forces that can harm them. Every wife is to be covered by a husband. Every child is to be covered by his or her parents. Many people hold positions of covering in everyday life because nothing was created to be without covering. The principal in the school is there to provide covering. The CEO of a major corporation is there to provide covering. The pastor of the local church is there to provide covering. If there were no one available to provide covering, the world in which we live would be one of chaos and confusion.

God recognized man's need for covering. Man was created to represent the Father's presence in the earth. Therefore, God Himself became a covering for mankind. He accepted this role even after man rejected His Lordship of his life. Today many men have become confused about their roles simply because they have decided to redefine their purposes. A man who fails to realize his responsibility to cover will also misrepresent what it means to be a man. Is it any surprise today that men are absent in the home? They are absent because manhood has been compromised to the point that men no longer realize that authentic manhood is reflected by fatherhood. No man can provide for his family or protect them from a distance. Whenever something lacks covering, it is exposed. It is vulnerable to attack, assault, or to the intents of an enemy.

Chapter 1

THESE WERE THE MEN WHO CAME

Understanding Leadership and Relationship

E very human being is in need of leadership. This is especially true for men because the perception is that they are supposed to lead. Historically men are to lead as the providers, protectors, and shepherds of their families. This challenge is by no means limited to men. Today many women have taken on the leadership role because there is no man in their situation. Leadership is not limited to gender. Be reminded that God made mankind male and female. He did not just make the male In similar fashion, He gave the responsibility of dominion and replenishing the earth to both of them. As a result, leadership represents common ground. This point, however, has less to do with leadership and more to do with relationship. Neither the man nor the woman could accomplish the will of God outside the context of relationship. In other words, it takes both the man and the woman to accomplish the purpose of God in the earth.

It is possible to become disillusioned about leadership in light of relationship. Often one is sacrificed for the other. Many relationships suffer because there is a lack of understanding pertaining to leadership. The fact is that everyone cannot be the leader. We all follow at some point and time in life, but leadership is a designated position that encompasses purpose. God has created everything with a purpose. Notice that when the created thing fulfilled the purpose for which it was created, God declared that it was "good." This is true since the fulfillment of purpose brings glory to God. In contrast, anything created that does not fulfill its purpose remains outside the will of God.

The Father addressed the leadership question. When God created man (male and female), the woman was in the man. Thus God reveals a leadership principle. Adam was touched by God alone, and as a result, received everything from his Creator. He understood his purpose and his role because the Father revealed it to him. There was no other source from which Adam could receive anything. This is very important for men to understand. Men are to receive their identities, their purposes, and their roles from their Creator. When men are touched by any source other than their heavenly Father, their relationship with God is compromised. God intended for man to be touched only by Him. As a result, God provides for all man's needs.

The True Responsibility for Leadership

This principle also works in the context of the man and the woman. The woman was in the man! Let's illustrate this point. When a woman becomes pregnant, the baby is in the woman. Everything the baby needs is supplied by the mother. Everything the baby receives is received from the mother. The mother serves as the only source of nourishment and life while the baby remains in her. The same principle is true for the woman. Eve was in Adam. Therefore everything Eve received, she received from the man. Adam was responsible to provide for the woman, to nourish and sustain her. The woman received everything from the man. Notice it was God who revealed the next step in order to fulfill His greater purpose. *The LORD God said, It is not good for the man to be alone. I will make a helper suitable for him* (Genesis 2:18).

In order for this to be accomplished, God had to remove the woman from the man. *So the LORD God caused the man to fall into a deep sleep; and while he was sleeping, He took one of the man's ribs and closed up the place with flesh. Then the LORD God made a woman from the rib He had taken out of the man, and He brought her to the man* (Genesis 2:21–22). It can be assumed that the man was still responsible for the woman, but he must now exercise his leadership in guiding, providing, and protecting her. This is where leadership is established and needed. Adam, having been touched by God, was to lead his wife according to the ways of God. This is his purpose. This is his role. In reality, this is his responsibility. God brought the woman to the man so that he might lead in this relationship. Adam was responsible to communicate the will of the Father to his family. The struggle faced today is how to restore men to their created place of leadership. God has not changed His mind concerning leadership, and He has not changed His position concerning man.

This is why all of mankind is in need of leadership. However, this speaks directly to the need for men to lead. Men must understand their purpose. They were designated and designed by God to provide leadership for their families. Please do not overlook the context of this revelation. "It is not good for the man to be alone." This is not simply referring to the physical aspect of relationship that we so quickly identify with. Rather, the impact of this is far greater. This affects all of life because it creates a leadership gap. The absence of the man in the context of the family has proven to be devastating. Whenever the man is missing from his appointed position, there are serious consequences in terms of order and authority. For example, when the woman is left in the position to be both the father and the mother, there comes a point in the process of rearing children when her authority is challenged, usually by a son. The natural result of this disrespect for her authority is the compromise of order. This is why the man is needed in the home. This is not meant to imply that children do not rebel against fathers, but it must be acknowledged that the transition to adulthood is smoother when there is a father in the home. This is true because the man's responsibility is to maintain order. The challenge today is that men have failed to realize the value of their touch upon the lives of those they are responsible to cover.

Leadership Requires an Example

Human beings must realize that they are not innately able to lead themselves. Though men have tried or created philosophies promoting their independence, history has proven that this dream has not yet been fulfilled. Every individual must have an example of leadership in his or her life. This is why we see the demand for leadership in every arena of life. There must be a principal for every school. There must be a mayor for every city and a governor for every state. This is why there are pastors for churches and CEOs for businesses. In short, there must be leadership. Any person or organization that lacks leadership is destined for confusion and ultimately for failure. There is no substitute for leadership. God

Himself is the leader of all creation. He is the One in authority who has the responsibility to maintain order. Paul wrote to the church at Corinth these words: *For God is not a God of disorder, but of peace* (1 Corinthians 14:33a). Verse 40, in this same chapter, reads: *But everything should be done in a fitting and orderly way.* This unmistakably infers that God is the leader of all creation and mankind. Man was created to live in God's Kingdom and to recognize His established order.

God alone is responsible for leading men. His heart is that men would recognize Him as King and submit to His will and purpose for their lives. God has given men a designated position in creation that represents a divine purpose. Men are to represent God as the examples of leadership to the family, providing vision and purpose in life. Men are to represent the Father as kings, prophets, and priests in their homes, providing spiritual covering for their wives and children. Men must provide emotional stability for those that they lead. Of course, the man received this direction from his Father. God serves as the source for all of man's identity and purpose. All men must work to avoid distraction and the compromise of their purpose in life. The failure of men to represent authority and maintain the order of God in their homes has consequences far beyond them. When Adam ate the forbidden fruit, everything changed. There was an immediate awareness that both the man and the woman were naked. When Adam disobeyed the Lord's command, his relationship with his Creator was forever compromised. Now things had changed in the eternal realm that could not be fixed by man himself. This was beyond his abilities. There are times in every life when one must realize that the situation or circumstance is beyond his or her ability to control. For example, a person can find himself in a position where someone else is making decisions that determine his actions. It was never God's will that man would find himself in a position where someone other than the Father would have control over his decisions. Man was created to represent dominion and authority in the earth and to become the blessing that would make this experience real in the lives of his family.

A Leadership Gap

The Book of Chronicles reveals a time when leadership was lacking. It is recorded that Saul was the first king of Israel. He came into office as a result of a leadership gap. When history is reviewed, it must be acknowledged that this leadership gap was long in the making. The children of Israel were chosen by God to represent His purpose in the earth. Furthermore, from their lineage God had promised a King whose kingdom would have no end. The problem, however, was that Israel was in bondage in the land of Egypt. God raised up Moses to be a leader for His people. Moses accepted the responsibility to obey God in leading the people of Israel from bondage in Egypt to the Promised Land prepared for them. Moses was blessed in spite of the people and was also influential in being an example of a father to Joshua. Joshua learned leadership from the example that Moses lived before him. In time Joshua replaced Moses as the leader of God's people. This is very important and is imperative for men to understand. Men must be committed to the challenge of preventing leadership gaps. Man must especially be discerning of his responsibility and role before God and ensure that he leads by example and imparts to his sons the spirit of David! This challenge to lead and to impart is real and is needed in the world today. God has called men to lead, and this revelation must be perpetuated from one generation to the next.

Two references from the Bible are necessary if one is to understand the seriousness of this revelation.

> *After these things, Joshua son of Nun, the servant of the LORD, died at the age of a hundred and ten. And they buried him in the land of his inheritance, at Timnath Serah in the hill country of Ephraim, north of Mount Gaash. Israel served the LORD throughout the lifetime of Joshua and of the elders who outlived him and who had experienced everything the LORD had done for Israel*
> —JOSHUA 24:29–31

> *The people served the LORD throughout the lifetime of Joshua and of the elders who outlived him and who had seen all the great things the LORD had done for Israel. Joshua son of Nun, the servant of the LORD, died at the age of a hundred and ten. And they buried him in the land of his inheritance, at Timnath Heres in the hill country of Ephraim, north of Mount Gaash. After that whole generation had been gathered to their ancestors, another generation grew up who knew neither the LORD nor what he had done for Israel. Then the Israelites did evil in the eyes of the LORD and served the Baals. They forsook the LORD, the God of their ancestors, who had brought them out of Egypt. They followed and worshiped various gods of the peoples around them. They aroused the LORD's anger.*
> —JUDGES 2:7–12

Sons and daughters were always meant to be taught lovingly by a father. As stated before, the father is responsible for order in the home. God, as the heavenly Father, established order through creation. He put His touch on all that was created. This simply means that God imparted life to everything He created. This is the responsibility of the father in the home. He must impart life to his sons and daughters. Sons will never become brothers who understand their role to cover others without impartation from a father. Sons will never mature into godly men who live by covenant promises realizing their very lives were meant to touch succeeding generations without the wise counsel of fathers.

Therefore, it is possible to lose an entire generation as a result of a leadership gap. It is explained vividly that a generation grew up that did not know the Lord or the great things that He had done for His people. This was simply the result of a lack of leadership and failure to impart vision and purpose to the succeeding generation. In addition, it is revealed that the Israelites did evil in the sight of the Lord and served the gods of those around them. Whenever there is a lack of leadership and impartation, the next generation will lose direction. One of the greatest struggles facing men today is a lack of direction concerning manhood. Many men really don't know what it means to be a man. The world increasingly attempts to redefine manhood for them, but they are lost in their quest for truth. Many men are limited and discouraged because they have never had a fatherly example in their lives, but manhood has been defined by the Creator, the Father of all men. God created man to be like Him in the earth. His heart is that men would walk in dominion providing the leadership necessary to represent and maintain His order in the earth. Men are "called" as leaders who are to sustain and expand the Kingdom of God in the earth. This is not a one-time calling, but an eternal calling that is to be established and imparted to all generations.

The leadership gap began with the death of Joshua and continued throughout the span of the judges, but God the Father is never content with leadership gaps. This is true because He is always the leader and wants His leadership represented in the earth. In order for this to be a reality, God uses mankind—men and women—to lead. Whenever there is a lack of leadership, God is preparing someone else to stand in the gap so that His purpose in the earth can be fulfilled.

Samuel the prophet represents one whom God raised up because there was a gap in leadership. Eli, the priest, who was called to provide leadership and covering for the people of God, was now old and struggling to maintain the order expected of him by the Lord. He also had sons who were evil in the sight of the Lord and did not exemplify the respect that was due to their earthly father or to their heavenly Father. As a result, God revealed to Samuel his calling to represent His authority and order in Israel. This point must not be missed or taken lightly. God is serious about leadership, and, therefore He is serious about finding a person who can represent His leadership in the earth. This is as much about representation as it is about leadership. God is about order and is committed to finding those men who can represent His established order. The Father does not have to redo anything He has done because He has done all things well. The problem is never with the Lord but with man. When Eli and his sons failed to represent God in an acceptable way, God initiated the process of preparing another man to represent Him. Men need to understand this principle. God's will is that every man would represent Him according to the purpose for which he was created. However, man's rebellion against God's established order does not negate His divine purpose. God will raise up another man or woman who will obey His Word and fulfill His purpose.

The result that God is looking for is always the same. This point is illustrated in 1 Samuel 3:19–20 which reads: *The LORD was with Samuel as he grew up, and He let none of Samuel's words fall to the ground. And all Israel from Dan to Beersheba recognized that Samuel was attested as a prophet of the LORD.* The true prophet of the Lord will never have to tell anyone that he is a prophet. The true prophet will be known by his works. The same is true with manhood. A true man will not have to tell anyone that he is a man. A true man will be known by his character. First, he will be known by the outpouring of the Lord within him. God is always with men who represent His order in the earth. When a man submits to the authority of the Father, he will be blessed! When a man surrenders his will to the will of his Father, he will experience increase. It is revealed that all of Israel acknowledged Samuel as a prophet of the Lord. When men walk in dominion according to the plan of God, all those that come in contact with them will recognize their authority. Authority is not something achieved as a result of position, gender, or status, but true authority is the fruit of God's touch upon one's life. Man was created to lead and has been anointed to walk in dominion. The anointing to lead is the result of a designated position in the order of God. In other words, men must lead because they will be held accountable. Men must lead because they have been given a designated role in the family. Their position and place represents the purpose of God, and His purposes will prevail. God anoints men who truly understand His plan in the earth.

One of the consequences of a leadership gap is rebellion against established authority. In the Book of 1 Samuel it is revealed that the children of Israel went to Samuel the prophet and requested a king like all the other nations had. *So all the elders of Israel gathered together and came to Samuel at Ramah. They said to him, "You are old, and your sons do not follow your ways; now appoint a king to lead us, such as all the other nations have"* (1 Samuel 8:4–5). Their request was made because there was a lack of leadership. It is obvious that Samuel had represented godly leadership up to this point. It is also evident that the elders of Israel expected Samuel's sons to follow in his example. In other words, Samuel represented God in leading the people. This fact was already understood. In contrast, his sons did not represent godly leadership, and all of Israel was aware of it.

Because of a leadership gap, the elders of Israel not only rejected Samuel's sons but also God. It was God who was King over Israel. He was their King, but because of a leadership gap, their hearts and eyes were turned away from the Lord, and they desired a king like all the other nations. Men have a divine responsibility to provide leadership for their homes and families that does not permit leadership gaps. In the absence of a father in the home, children will seek a father's touch elsewhere. This is being witnessed in many neighborhoods and cities in our nation today. Youth, especially young men, continue to look for fatherly affirmation outside the home. This tragic reality can only be resolved as a result of men returning to their designated place of leadership. Failure to address leadership gaps will only perpetuate this dilemma and result in additional generations being lost to counterfeit sources of leadership.

Rejecting God as King

Does it concern anyone today that this problem continues to escalate and no one seems to notice the true problem? When the elders came to Samuel with their solution, they had not discerned that they were also rejecting divine leadership in the process. It was Samuel alone who had a problem with their request because he understood the spiritual implications and the potential ramifications.

But when they said, "Give us a king to lead us," this displeased Samuel;
so he prayed to the LORD. And the LORD told him: "Listen to all that
the people are saying to you; it is not you they have rejected, but they
have rejected me as their king."

—1 SAMUEL 8:6–7

The world continues to reject the leadership of God as King while all the time desiring the kings of this world. Like Samuel, men must be sensitive to the fact they have been appointed to lead. Their responsibility is to maintain the Father's authority in the earth and to safeguard His divine order. Men are failing to touch their own sons in ways that ensure the continuation of godly order in the earth. There is no alternative solution to this challenge. The restoration of the man will be the result of fatherly and godly leadership in these last days.

Every father's goal must be to impart these godly principles to his sons and other men. There must be no leadership gaps. Men must make this responsibility their priority because the consequence is a lost generation. God is also committed to this proposition. First Chronicles 10 reveals that the Philistines were at war with Israel.

Now the Philistines fought against Israel; the Israelites fled before
them, and many fell dead on Mount Gilboa. The Philistines were in
hot pursuit of Saul and his sons, and they killed his sons Jonathan,
Abinadab and Malki-Shua. The fighting grew fierce around Saul,
and when the archers overtook him, they wounded him.

—1 CHRONICLES 10:1–3

The Bible reveals that Saul and all his sons were killed in one day. The death of the king created a leadership gap not only in the present but also for the future. There was no son left to sit on the throne of his father. It is obvious that God was moving to ensure that Israel would have a king to lead them. The position of king was important to God because the king was to represent His Lordship in the earth. David had gained his fame as a result of slaying Goliath, a giant who represented the army of the Philistines and defiled the God of Israel. Saul, as king of Israel, had failed to provide the leadership necessary to overcome the assault of the enemy.

In addition, he seemed to have missed the opportunity to impart into the lives of his own sons their responsibility to represent God's order in the earth. David realized he was created to walk in dominion and to defend the battleground of the Lord from the enemy. The spirit of David is heard as he cries: *Who is this uncircumcised Philistine that he should defy the armies of the living God?* (1 Samuel 17:26b). At this time, David had become a person of notoriety who served under King Saul as an officer in the army of Israel. He found favor with God, and the Lord had exalted him in the eyes of all Israel. But because of Saul's jealousy, David found himself on the run. But now Saul and all his sons had been killed in battle. There was no king in Israel, and the leadership gap needed to be filled as quickly as possible. The whole nation was without leadership. Another generation of men could not be lost. God took the responsibility to identify a leader and to exalt him in the eyes of the nation of Israel. David had been chosen by God to shepherd His people and to teach them about the true King and His Kingdom.

Although every man and woman has been created to lead and to walk in dominion, this will never become a reality without an example. In other words, in the same way one learns everything else, leadership must also be learned. Man is born dependent and therefore must have someone to nurture and guide him to maturity. An example is required. God, as Creator, is the ultimate example of leadership. He is the supreme leader and is qualified to teach all creation about leadership. He is in control of all things, and He alone can direct life's pathway in order to accomplish His purpose and plan for each life. There is no greater leader than God. There is no better leader than the Lord. Sons today cannot afford to make the mistakes of their fathers. Men today must confess their need for leadership and acknowledge that God is the leader of all creation. Failure to agree with this point only implies that men are in rebellion, still believing they are able to solve their own problems and have the authority themselves to navigate their own futures. Men must accept the responsibility to impart to their sons what it really means to be a man! This can only be accomplished by fathers touching sons, sons touching brothers, and brothers touching one another. Whenever there is a leadership gap, those who follow will seek a leader.

> *All Israel came together to David at Hebron and said, "We are your own flesh and blood. In the past, even while Saul was king, you were the one who led Israel on their military campaigns. And the LORD your God said to you, 'You will shepherd my people Israel, and you will become their ruler.'" When all the elders of Israel had come to King David at Hebron, he made a covenant with them at Hebron before the LORD, and they appointed David king over Israel, as the LORD had promised through Samuel.*
>
> —1 CHRONICLES 11:1–3

The Anointing of Manhood

David had been identified by God as the next king in Israel. This had been confirmed by the prophet Samuel who had gone to David's father's house and anointed David with oil as king. All of this transpired before

David ever became king. God, however, was preparing David for kingship. This is absolutely critical. Regardless of the people men have in their lives, they must be prepared for manhood by their heavenly Father. God will always use parents and other men in their lives to impart to them godly truths that will help them mature and respect their identities and purposes in life, but the anointing of manhood must come from their true Father. This anointing is necessary because it was God who created man and gave him his identity and purpose for life. Like David, men must come to realize that in spite of their daily challenges, God has a far greater purpose for their being here on this earth.

Men can only find fulfillment in allegiance to their true King. God is a generational God, and often the purpose for a man's life is to be fulfilled in his seed or by others into whom he has imparted vision. This is why leadership is so important. God never intended for His vision to die with a man. This is even true of His own Son, Jesus Christ, who died for the sins of humankind. Though He came to die, He also came to birth the church. This required leadership and His life is a testimony of what it means to pour a vision into others. Paul shared this revelation in 2 Timothy 2:2: *And the things you have heard me say in the presence of many witnesses entrust to reliable people who will also be qualified to teach others.* Paul identified the challenge. Each father must be committed to teach his sons the truths of God's Word and their role in fulfilling His will. Every man must see himself as a brother to every other man. Together, they must remain faithful to the command to perpetuate the meaning of true manhood to each succeeding generation.

Why Men Came to David

The question must be raised: Why did men come to David? The rationale for this question comes from 1 Chronicles 12:1–2, which reads: *These were the men who came to David at Ziklag, while he was banished from the presence of Saul son of Kish (they were among the warriors who helped him in battle; they were armed with bows and were able to shoot arrows or to sling stones right-handed or left-handed; they were relatives of Saul from the tribe of Benjamin).*

These men were the kinsmen of King Saul. They obviously were aware of Saul's disposition towards David. Saul was jealous of David and had made numerous attempts on his life. The motive for this stemmed from the fact that David had been anointed to be the next king in Israel, and this was known by Saul. The problem with this situation is a most common one. Saul was still king, and one cannot have two kings. *Saul was afraid of David, because the LORD was with David but had departed from Saul* (1 Samuel 18:12). Apparently, Saul wanted to remain king for all the wrong reasons. Is it possible that Saul thought that killing David would result in his regaining the anointing and favor of God? The favor of God comes with purpose and calling but also must be accompanied by obedience and sacrifice. There is a price that comes with leadership.

Manhood is often misunderstood. It has been said that just because one is a male does not automatically mean that one is a man. Manhood is something that is achieved first as revelation from God. It requires an impartation that must be nurtured and then affirmed. Even Jesus needed the affirmation of His Father. Every man—in fact, every individual— needs the affirmation of a father. Jesus followed the example of His Father and, because of His obedience, was affirmed by His Father. The affirmation of a father cements the purposes of the sons or daughters and provides spiritual covering for their lives and futures. This is evident in the Old Testament where fathers oftentimes blessed their sons who were to receive the mantle of anointing necessary to fulfill the promises of God in their lives. Thus it was understood that leadership was necessary and that the passing of the torch demanded the affirmation of the father.

Why did men come to David? These men, a band of brothers, were seeking affirmation. They had been exposed to a model of leadership that provided little or no opportunity for the next generation. Saul failed to affirm David. He obviously had not affirmed his own sons. Now these men came to David seeking the very thing they had been denied by Saul. When Saul died there was a shifting of the anointing. God will not anoint disobedience. First Chronicles 10:13–14 reveals: *Saul died because he was unfaithful to the LORD; he did not keep the word of the LORD and even consulted a medium for guidance, and did not inquire of the LORD. So the LORD put him to death and turned the kingdom over to David son of Jesse.* Everyone needs leadership. Put another way, everyone needs a father's touch. No one is exempt from the need for an example in his or her life, the affirmation of his or her purpose, the confirmation of his or her identity, and the spiritual covering over his or her life and future.

This is especially true for men today. Men are drawn to leadership because they are seeking the confirmation of their identities and the affirmation of their purposes. Manhood must be both taught and caught. The ability to create a baby does not qualify one as a man. The test of manhood is the ability to raise children and to be an example, nurturing them to a place of maturity where they are not confused about their identities or purposes. Men must have a leader because they learn to lead by example. Leadership must be exemplified before them so that they know what leadership is. The same is true with fatherhood. Where else can young men learn about fatherhood except from fathers? This is why the Word declares that we *do not have many [spiritual] fathers* (1 Corinthians 4:15).

Men are looking for spiritual fathers. Men are searching for spiritual direction and truth, and all men will follow after the anointing because they, too, need it in their own lives. It is no small thing that these men were among those who helped Saul in battle. Men will be willing to go to battle for the anointing. They will stand with and stand by a leader who has been called and anointed by God to impart truth into their lives. Men will follow those who have touched their lives.

Chapter 2

THE COVERING
OF A FATHER

How Important Is This?

ollowing is a sample of what sources have to say about the risks faced by fatherless children:

- 63 percent of youth suicides are from fatherless homes (U.S. Dept. of Health and Human Services, Bureau of the Census)

- 85 percent of all children that exhibit behavioral disorders come from fatherless homes (Centers for Disease Control)

- 80 percent of rapists motivated with displaced anger come from fatherless homes (*Criminal Justice & Behavior*, Vol. 14, p. 403–26, 1978)

- 71 percent of all high school dropouts come from fatherless homes (National Principals Association Report on the State of High Schools)

- 70 percent of juveniles in state-operated institutions come from fatherless homes (U.S. Dept. of Justice, Special Report, Sept. 1988)

- 85 percent of all youths sitting in prisons grew up in a fatherless home (Fulton Co. Georgia jail populations, Texas Dept. of Corrections, 1992)*

How Important Is This?

In an age where more and more fathers are absent in the home, how important is the covering of a father? The role of fatherhood is changing so fast and being redefined so quickly that most people are not even aware of the changes. The average home today is perceived as a single-parent home, usually led by the mother. In fact, the general rule in the home is to prepare daughters for independence. This does not mean that she may not marry, but that she should not be solely dependent on any man.

We live in a world where philosophies and principles of life are being written and re-written at a staggering pace. The tragic end of this reality is that men and women, boys and girls, are being exposed to these new mentalities without any foundation of truth upon which to stand. It is evident that world views are changing, and recent generations have been affected more than previously realized. Even the family is being redefined, and many of these new definitions do not include a father. This shift in perception is the result of divorce, unwed mothers, and a consistent rise in the number of singles who never marry. There are additional factors that have contributed to this transition, but the result is always the same: the absence of fathers in the home has become a social epidemic.

Another more subtle shift that has even more devastating effects on the home is the father who is home but does not impact the family. He

---

* "Fatherless Homes Breed Violence," http://www.fathermag.com/ (accessed May 14, 2014).

is home but not available. He is present but not engaged. His idea of fatherhood is simply to provide. He has been subconsciously taught that the role of the man is to work and to provide "things" for his family. The result of this teaching still fosters a leadership gap! In spite of the fact that the man is in the home, he provides no vision and has no spiritual agenda. For example, he sends his family to church but usually does not attend himself. He holds a position but provides no tangible leadership that is productive to the welfare and growth of his family.

He appears to be a leader by his presence but fails to lead by his actions. He is often unable to support family events because of the priority of work. In similar fashion, he rarely touches the lives of his children but still demands their respect. He provides little, if any, support to his wife in correcting his children but becomes upset when he feels his wife does not honor him. It is no small wonder that young men are struggling with the concept of manhood. It should not be a surprise that many teenage males struggle with their own identities and are confused about their sexuality and their roles as men. What does it mean to be a man? How do you know when you have become a man? Is the answer to these questions as simple as reaching a certain age in life? If manhood is arrived at chrono-logically, then every male man would have reached manhood. However, the sad reality is there are many older men who have not matured in life and cannot serve as an example of true manhood. There are as many unacceptable perceptions of manhood as there are inappropriate examples to follow. It has been said before and must be repeated again: "Everything male is not a man." The true definition and role model of manhood must be restored. For example, gang violence continues to take its toll in lives as many youth in communities die committed to a concept of manhood that demands hardness and loyalty to a counterfeit family.

Based on law enforcement reports, it is estimated that in 2009, there were 28,100 gangs and 731,000 gang members throughout 3,500 jurisdictions in the United States…The number of jurisdictions with gang problems and the number of gangs increased more than 20 percent from 2002 to 2009, with both indicators recording a 5 percent increase in more recent years.*

This is largely the result of a leadership gap and the fact that many of these young men have never been affirmed by a natural or spiritual father. Many other young men have been distracted by greed and lust, believing this is what manhood is really all about. More and more of these young men have been lured away at earlier ages while the family seems unable to respond appropriately and receives little or no apparent support from the church. If fathers are absent from the home and mothers turn to the church only to find that fathers are absent there as well, how can these mothers find the answers so desperately needed to the challenges of raising sons in today's society? What does it mean to be a man?

The apostle Paul provides insight into this dilemma. He writes: *When I was a child, I talked like a child, I thought like a child, I reasoned like a child. When I became a man, I put the ways of childhood behind me* (1 Corinthians 13:11). Childhood represents a totally different mindset than adulthood. In other words, one can discern the lack of maturity in a child by the way he thinks. Paul reveals that the immature male thinks like a child. Children think in terms of their needs. When they are hungry, they want to know what's for dinner or when dinner will be ready. They have no need to be concerned about where the food comes from or how much it

---

* Highlights of the 2009 National Youth Gang Survey, Office of Juvenile Justice and Delinquency Prevention, 2011.

costs. They remain unaware of the fact the food must be prepared. They simply want to sit down and eat! When dinner is over, they want to go and play. When they are tired, they refuse to go to bed because they have no concept of responsibility. There is, in essence, no reason why they need to go to bed. They don't need rest in order to prepare for work the next day. This is absolutely foreign to them.

Parents must help their children visualize adulthood. For example, the responsibility of parents is to slowly expose their children to all the realities associated with dinner. Parents often begin by asking them to set the table or to help clean up after dinner. Parents may increase the children's awareness by including them in the preparation of the meal itself or by taking them shopping with them to the supermarket to actually purchase the food. Parents rarely start out by asking a child to pay for the meal because this request would be unreasonable. But slowly the parents continue exposing the child to the bigger picture, helping him to understand there is a process associated to the dinner meal. They also are teaching him responsibility at varying levels with the ultimate lesson of taking responsibility for providing his own dinner. The end result involves the hope that he will one day provide dinner for someone besides himself. The pathway to manhood demands an impartation that as a man he will one day provide dinner for his own family.

The difference between childhood and adulthood is not simply an awareness of the bigger picture. Paul emphatically declares that when he became a man, he put childish ways behind him. This simply meant he no longer thought from a child's perspective. As an adult, as a father, he still begins from the position of need but realizes his responsibility and role is to see that the needs of others are met. This is just like the heavenly Father. He has promised to provide for all of man's needs. Nothing is too big for Him. Following God's example, a mature man thinks differently. He anticipates the needs of his family and begins drafting plans to take care of them. A mature man must first realize that there are needs beyond just the physical spheres of food and shelter. A mature man understands that the greatest needs of his family are spiritual. He comprehends that he must play a major role in providing guidance and instruction for his family so they understand their identities and purposes in light of the will of God.

He prayerfully discerns that he must provide instruction concerning finances. He must be the example in his own home of stewardship. Stewardship is definitely not limited just to finances, but finances serve as the best test of one's stewardship because they represent sacrifice and priorities. God must be honored first. This is a strategic lesson that every father can share with his family. This responsibility is great because the father must cast the vision of stewardship for his wife. She is the senior partner, and children will never experience success with their finances until both the husband and wife demonstrate the value of teamwork and commitment to a greater vision. The inability of the husband and wife to walk in agreement concerning their finances is definitely one of the major reasons marriages are compromised. The adult man must think differently. The father must see beyond the present moment. There are many needs that his family will have. Some of them may involve transportation while others may be medical. The mature man must take into consideration the educational needs of his children and make preparation to provide for those needs. More importantly, he must impart to his own children the value of an education and the benefits of academic achievement.

The mature man arrives at manhood when he comprehends he must have a vision and a plan. He must lead because he is responsible and has accepted his responsibility as a provider. Proverbs 22:6 declares: *Train up a child in the way he should go, and when he is old he will not depart from it* (NKJV). Using the analogy of a train for a moment, picture a train with every car connected and running on the same track. The father is like the engine and is responsible to see that every car connected to him reaches the appointed destination. The father must lead by example because each car following him must travel the same path that he has gone. He must always be aware of his witness and responsibility to represent his heavenly Father to his family. There can be no shortcuts. If he finds himself derailed, all the other cars will follow. They will be affected by his success or failure. Therefore, a mature man must be involved, engaged, and encouraging because he will be accountable for the mental and emotional lives of his family. A real man thinks differently!

Fatherhood and Purpose

Fatherhood is a priority with God! He serves as the example to every earthly father of what true fatherhood really looks like. Regardless of the changes experienced in the earth, God has not changed His mind. Men must understand their roles in light of the Father's creative purpose. God does not create anything without a purpose. Purpose is important because it provides direction. Purpose addresses the question, "Why?." With this in mind, God desires to nurture His children until they understand their callings or purposes in life. The Father's heart is to cover His own until they discover their giftings and become committed to maximizing their potential. One maximizes his potential when he realizes where he was created to fit in this life. The place where a person fits is also the place where he can make his contribution.

This is paramount to fathering. Men must prayerfully seek the will of God concerning their wives and children. Fathers must faithfully pursue God's purpose for each child. The father must lead by providing covering and direction for his children. He must discern each child's gifting by participating in the fulfillment of his or her destiny. Likewise, this is important in marriage. God created the wife to be "a helpmeet" for her husband. In other words, the will of God in creating woman was that she would complete the man. This is an awesome calling and must be understood in the context of purpose. Failure to interpret the relationship in light of purpose will result in the wife competing with her husband. This is contrary to the will of the Creator and will prove counterproductive to the relationship. Both the husband and the wife must pursue one another's purposes and nurture each other's giftings so that each walks in maturity. This will produce a blessed relationship in which each spouse contributes to the health and well-being of the other.

Everything done in life is done in the context of relationships. There is nothing that men do outside the context of relationships. The English poet John Donne said it best: "No man is an island." No man stands alone. God has revealed many truths to men concerning the power of relationships. For example, the Word states: *One witness is not enough to convict anyone accused of any crime or offense they may have committed. A matter must be established by the testimony of two or three witnesses* (Deuteronomy 19:15). Notice God does not leave the verdict to one person. His preferred will is that there would be collaboration or agreement before a matter is settled. Amos, the minor prophet, expressed the concept this way: *Do two walk together unless they have agreed to do so?* (Amos 3:3). The King James Version phrases it this way: *Can two walk together, except they be agreed?* This is an important principle and speaks to the necessity for unity and oneness in relationships. It is possible to be married but not walk in unity. This verse emphasizes agreement and elevates it to a position of priority in every relationship. Unity must be legitimately represented if two people are to become one. Many married couples struggle to agree on anything. One may deduce that any marriage relationship would be better if the spouses walked in agreement. Too many couples experience failure because priority is placed on defense of their individual positions rather than seeking common ground upon which they can agree. Defending individual positions will always limit the growth of relationships.

Unlike mankind, God is always in agreement. The Father never contradicts Himself. Why is this true? It is true because God is first in agreement with His Word. Men and women struggle to walk in agreement with each other because they have not agreed to walk according to the Word of God. The Word of God represents truth and liberation! It is difficult to attempt to agree with someone else when that person is not free from deception and has no foundation of truth on which to rely. If men themselves, define truth, there will be as many definitions as there are people. Simply put, people cannot be the measure of truth because they constantly change. They change their decisions. They change their positions. They change their minds. If something is to be the measure of truth, it must remain constant. It must weather the seasons of time. The Bible reveals that God does not change. Malachi 3:6 declares: *I the LORD do not change.* Because God does not change, He is the best representative of truth. His motives do not change. He has no personal agenda that would compromise His integrity. He is the eternal Father and is committed to His purpose for mankind. Man will always benefit when he obeys the Father's will for his life.

The challenge for man is to think like God thinks. Remember: a child thinks from the perspective of need. The child is driven by his own need. All too often even grown men and women are driven solely by their needs. This represents deception and is one of the major weapons used by the enemy to distract men from the will of God. If a child is to become an adult, his way of thinking must change. How does God think? He thinks from the perspective of truth. God cannot lie! *God is not a human, that He should lie, not a human being, that He should change His mind. Does He speak and then not act? Does He promise and not fulfill?* (Numbers 23:19). The challenge for men, in the context of relationships, is to be led by truth. This implies the man must learn to lead according to God's revealed purpose and plan for his life. Furthermore, he must lead based on the revelation of the Father's will for his family. He follows the path already established by God's Word and is committed to imparting these truths to his children. In order for a man to lead his family, he must be a student of the Word of God because truth is only found in God's Word. Men are accountable to God to take the lead in representing and sharing truth with those they are destined to cover.

Men desperately need fathers who have their best interest at heart. They are hungry for fathers who will share with them practical realities and lessons learned from their own lives. Men desire examples that share not only their victories but also their struggles and sometimes their failures. In similar fashion, men have proven they desire fathers who provide covering of direction and guidance as they face the challenges of life. Above all, men must have spiritual fathers who reveal to them their heavenly Father. There is no greater gift a father can give to his son than to usher him into adulthood in right relationship with his Creator. This represents an eternal blessing because when earthly fathers are no longer present in this life they will perpetually live on in the hearts and lives of sons who have sat at their feet and been sharpened. The purpose of fatherhood involves sharing the truths of life with children, especially sons, and letting them know that life is about more than just material gain.

Relationships Between Fathers and Sons

In the Book of 1 Samuel, chapter 16 begins this way: *The LORD said to Samuel, "How long will you mourn for Saul, since I have rejected him as king over Israel? Fill your horn with oil and be on your way; I am sending you to Jesse of Bethlehem. I have chosen one of his sons to be king."* A number of conclusions can be drawn from this single verse. First, Samuel the prophet was still mourning for Saul. The assumption is that Samuel was disappointed in Saul's failure to obey the command of the Lord. This was not just limited to his obvious disobedience concerning the Amalekites, but also involved his misrepresentation of the Lord before Israel. In other words, Saul, like so many other men, had the responsibility to represent God's order before His people. Men were created in the image and likeness of God. As a result, man is responsible to reflect who God is or to mirror the heart and mind of God to others. If sons are to know what it means to be men, then their fathers must be examples they can mirror. Sons must be taught the heart and mind of manhood. In similar fashion, the man was created in the likeness of God. This too is important because men need to know what God is like. What does God represent? What are His standards? How does God act? What is the character of God? These are questions that must be addressed if sons are to fulfill their destinies as men. Someone must respond to these questions if sons and brothers alike are to exemplify the character of their heavenly Father.

What does God represent? It has already been revealed that God represents truth. A high premium is placed on truth because God uses truth to set men free. This is the nature of the Father. It has always been His intention to first reveal Himself to man and then to have man represent or mirror His image to others. This is how God desires to be known. He wants men to be witnesses of His truth in the earth. God is also a righteous God. He is a moral being who represents what is right and wills that all creation would benefit from being right and then doing right. This is why we are called to treat one another in the same manner we want to be treated. The world is full of sin, and sin represents disorder. Wherever sin is present, things tend to be out of order. Man's responsibility is to maintain God's order in the earth. After all, the Father gave man the responsibility to walk in dominion. This is why it is so important for the man to lead because his purpose is to provide covering for others.

Wise people often say, "You cannot lead where you have not been, you cannot tell what you do not know, and you cannot share what you do not have." A leader must be ahead of the people he is leading! The man must accept the responsibility and call to be the spiritual leader of his house. He must understand this is a spiritual battle and souls are at stake. The point is that some of these souls are his responsibility. Men must be responsible for their own homes ensuring that their family members are not bound by the enemy. Finally, men must be good stewards. One of the major responsibilities of a steward is to realize that everything he has is but a trust from God. No man begins as an independent person. Children receive covering and nurture from parents until they are able to make it on their own. Husbands and wives build a life together so they can perpetuate themselves through their children, fulfilling the plan of God to multiply and fill the earth. But this responsibility also includes providing guidance, pointing the children in the right direction, and sharing with them truth so they mature in their quest to do right and avoid wrong.

What are His standards? This is a very good question because it has a lot to do with how God has revealed Himself to man. God wants men to know Him. He desires that His presence would be represented in the earth. All creation reflects God presence, but in order for men to appreciate God's presence, they must accept His standards. The Bible reveals that God's standard is the law. God revealed Himself to His people by giving them the Ten Commandments. This was God's formal way of introducing Himself to His people, Israel. *I am the LORD your God, who brought you out of Egypt, out of the land of slavery. You shall have no other gods before me* (Exodus 20:2–3). It is also His way of revealing what He expects from His people. Men struggle with the law. This is probably because men, in and of themselves, are not able to keep the law, but the real problem is not the law itself. God gave the law to protect man. The role of the law is to represent the standards of the Father. If one breaks the law, the same law condemns the lawbreaker. However, if one does not break the law, then the law protects him.

Fundamentally speaking, laws are created because someone does something that he should not do. Thus, a law is created to protect others from the same thing being done to them. This is why the only people who go to jail should be those convicted of breaking the law. Because of sin (sin nature), man's ability to live according to the Father's standards have been greatly compromised. As a result, God sent His only Son, Jesus, into the world to represent His standard when all others had failed. In other words, Jesus was the only man able to live His life in a way that was acceptable to the Father. Man's ability to meet the expectations of the Father are the result of grace—what God has done for man that he could not do for himself. God gave His only Son as a sacrifice for man's failures. The sacrificial death of Jesus paid the price for all men's failures and provides an opportunity for men to be restored in right relationship with their Creator. This happens by faith. Men must accept God's sacrificial gift and believe that Jesus died for their sins. Jesus represents God's standard now in the earth. The only way to the Father is through the Son. If men want to know the standard of the Father they need only seek the Son.

How does God act? Chancellor Oral Roberts declared that "God is a good God." This means that God can only act one way. It is His nature to do good. That is simply who He is. In other words, God is naturally good. This means that good is what He naturally does. This point must be illustrated. Birds naturally fly. Fish naturally swim. Humans naturally sin! If men were allowed to do whatever they wanted to do without any consequences, most likely they would sin. They would do wrong. Please do not minimize this revelation. All men struggle with doing good because they must realize that before they can do good they must become good. This is a problem for mankind. Paul, the apostle, shares a truth with men to which every man can relate.

> *We know that the law is spiritual; but I am unspiritual, sold as a slave to sin. I do not understand what I do. For what I want to do I do not do, but what I hate I do. And if I do what I do not want to do, I agree that the law is good. As it is, it is no longer I myself who do it, but it is sin living in me. For I know that good itself does not dwell in me, that is, in my sinful nature. For I have the desire to do what is good, but I cannot carry it out. For I do not do the good I want to do, but the evil I do not want to do—this I keep on doing.*

Now if I do what I do not want to do, it is no longer I who do it, but it is sin living in me that does it.

—Romans 7:14–20

Every man struggles with how to do right while avoiding wrong. This is why the concepts gleaned from studying the life of David is so important. He is described as a man after God's own heart, but he was yet human in that he was not perfect, but flawed. Romans 12:21 states: *Do not be overcome by evil, but overcome evil with good.* The fact remains evil is present always and is determined to overcome men. The problem men face is that the good needed to overcome evil is not within them. David faced this same reality in his life. Even after he failed, he had to realize he needed something beyond his natural limitations, something more than the mistakes he made. In reality, it needed to be life-transforming to the point where he would not make the same mistake again.

The next assumption drawn from 1 Samuel 16 reveals that God had rejected Saul as king over His people, Israel. Saul was no longer able to represent God as the fatherly covering over Israel. There is a correlation between the positions of king and father. The enemy has deceived men into thinking that they can be kings without being fathers. Fathering represents the very heart of God. Though He is the King of kings, He is always Father. One thing must be understood about the Lord. He will not allow anyone to compromise His glory! He demands reverence just because of who He is. He desires to use men to represent His ways in the earth. It must be understood that this requires obedience.

Saul's problem was arrogance. He became bigger than life in his own eyes. God had commanded Saul to attack and destroy the Amalekites for the way they had mistreated Israel when they came up from Egypt. Saul was to destroy every living thing. He was not to spare any living soul— men, women, children, or infants. In fact, Saul was even to destroy all livestock. Notice that God gave these instructions to Saul, and he was to represent God's will to the people. This was a test of leadership, and God expected Saul to lead. Personal leadership has to do with obedience while corporate leadership is always about vision. God does not just look at what one does in obedience, but also the way in which one does it. This has to do with the ability of the leader to cast God's vision to the people. Saul was to destroy the Amalekites and leave nothing alive. Did Saul have the heart of God as his sole priority? Saul wanted so much to be king that he forgot about being a father.

One test of a true leader is whether he will obey the Lord even in the midst of peer pressure. Saul obviously succumbed to the pressure of the people by allowing them to return with the best of the livestock. This disobedience was further complicated by the fact that Saul spared Agag, king of the Amalekites, and brought him back. Saul was deceived and felt he had done everything the Lord had commanded of him. When confronted by Samuel, he blamed the people. The problem with this response was the fact that he was the leader. No father is to be led by his children. If Saul had led in obedience, he would never have been in this position. Samuel shared the Father's reply to King Saul:

> *Does the LORD delight in burnt offerings and sacrifices as much as in obeying the LORD? To obey is better than sacrifice, and to heed is better than the fat of rams. For rebellion is like the sin of divination, and arrogance like the evil of idolatry. Because you have rejected the Word of the LORD, He has rejected you as king.*
> —1 SAMUEL 15:22–23

God described Saul's disobedience as rebellion and arrogance. It must be the priority of men to obey the Word of the Lord. This must begin in the heart and then manifest in one's pursuit of the Father's will. Because Saul's heart was not after God, he was rejected by the Father as king over Israel.

Finally, notice God sent Samuel to Bethlehem because he had already chosen the next king of Israel. Remember that God does not tolerate leadership gaps. He will always have a remnant in the earth—those who are totally committed to His Word. If a man fails to obey His command and becomes arrogant and rebellious, that man forfeits the favor of God on his life. This also results in the removal of that man from whatever position of leadership he had that represented the Father's heart to others. It is sad that Saul held selfishness and pride in greater priority than the submission of his heart to the will of his Heavenly Father.

Knowing the Heart of God

It is often said that Israel knew the will of God, but Moses knew His ways. What does it mean to know the ways of God? Jesus provides the answer to this question with this revelation: *"Why do you call me, Lord, Lord, and do not do what I say?"* (Luke 6:46). In other words, the will and the ways of God are one and the same. In Psalm 119:9–11, a question is raised and answered. The answer is important: *How can a young person stay on the path of purity? By living according to your word. I seek you with all my heart; do not let me stray from your commands.*

These verses again demonstrate the singleness of the will and way of God. The writer desires to keep his way pure. This literally means he wants to keep his heart right. This is accomplished by living according to the Word of God. The writer continues by declaring his sincere desire is to hide the Father's Word in his heart. The result of this commitment empowers him to not sin against God. The man that lives according to the Word of God and truly hides His Word in his heart is more likely to walk in obedience. Matthew, in his gospel, shares this insight: *For where your treasure is, there your heart will be also"* (Matthew 6:21). When God becomes a man's treasure, that man's heart will be captured by His Word.

The Father is seeking after this kind of man. These are the kinds of fathers that sons need. These are the kinds of leaders for which the world is looking. Yes, these are even the kinds of husbands for which wives are praying. The world is full of men who are being rejected by their heavenly Father. Too many men, like Saul, have allowed rebellion and pride to overshadow the Father's heart in their lives. Far too many sons have succumbed to the pressures and influences of this present age. They lack the example of a true father and, as a result, have no true perception of manhood. In similar fashion, too many sons have followed after false images and negative portrayals of manhood. They have compromised their potential by submitting to the pressures of their environment.

Saul was called to be a leader. Saul's purpose as king was to represent the Lordship of the Father to the nation he was now responsible to lead. These men desperately needed a godly leader, a spiritual father in their lives. The sad reality is men need leaders too! The challenge faced in this current day is that young men are not able to identify their leaders. Sons are not able to identify their own fathers. In addition, many sons who know their fathers do not respect them because they have never truly touched their lives when they needed it most. Far too many sons are entering adulthood without ever having been prepared for manhood. Thus we are not surprised that young men today have failed to duplicate the examples of generations passed. It has been said that an entire generation of young men have already been lost. There is much work to do to abort this trend and rescue the men of the future from the snares of today.

If one was to meditate seriously about the transition of the family, he might realize that just two generations ago the challenges faced today did not exist. In contrast, it was normal to have a father in the home. Marriages were the norm, and divorce was the exception. In fact, many couples, known as great-grandparents and grandparents, were married for over fifty years. It is more than a challenge to find marriages today that have survived the test of time. Teenage pregnancy was not a social crisis. Those days of the past were characterized by mature children who valued family and assumed responsibility, understanding the simple truth that hard work was necessary and sacrifice was required. Think about it—parents have always spoiled their children, but the children of those parents did not have the entitlement mentality of youth today. The children representing past generations were accustomed to hand-me-downs, and everything did not have to be new. These are real problems demanding real answers.

The absence of fathers in the home and the confusion surrounding manhood only adds to this crisis. If this present onslaught is to be turned back, it will demand the restoration of the male man. Once again fathers must take their place in the home, and men must take their places in the church, in the workplace, and in society at large. Simply put, men must again find their purposes and realize their identities. This can only be accomplished by example and nurturing. May the Father of all mankind move quickly to anoint and raise up the next generations of "Davids" who are to replace and correct the failures of a generation of "Sauls." This was the cry of the Old Testament prophet Malachi who proclaimed the heart of the eternal God when he wrote:

Remember the law of my servant Moses, the decrees and laws I gave him at Horeb for all Israel. See, I will send the prophet Elijah to you before that great and dreadful day of the LORD comes. He will turn the hearts of the parents to their children, and the hearts of the children to their parents; or else I will come and strike the land with a curse.

—MALACHI 4:4–6

David As an Example

It is obvious that David grew up in the background of his older brothers. He was never considered a leader because of his age. Even as his brother got older, the fact that he was also aging was never a factor considered in his own development as a man. His father, Jesse, was apparently proud of all his sons, but when it came to a father's covering, David simply found himself outside of this father's consciousness. This is nowhere more apparent than when his family was visited by the prophet Samuel. When the sons of Jesse were presented before the prophet of God, David was not only absent but forgotten as well. Regardless of the rationale, this did not appear to be a one-time oversight but rather a reoccurring tragedy. David found himself outside the covering of his father. Had he gotten accustomed to always being an afterthought?

Far too many sons and daughters have asked this same question today. When they attempt to surmise the priorities of their fathers, they are consistently confronted with the possibility that they too have been forgotten. In their confusion they misunderstand their need for a father's covering from their fathers. Because of their frustration, they find themselves distanced from fathers who find the time for work but never find quality time for them. How can sons be expected to uphold the priority to cover their families as fathers when they have never experienced being covered themselves? It is apparent that David suffered in his later years as a father with his own sons. Could his struggle with his own children be the expected manifestation of a wound that never healed? Men and fathers must be awakened to their need to provide covering for their children. Sons must have an example of fatherhood that covers if they are to one day provide covering for their own children. There is no acceptable alternative for men who fail manhood, husbands who abandon covenant relationships, or fathers who consistently miss the opportunities to affirm their sons and daughters. The simple truth remains. There is an unrelenting need for a father's covering.

Chapter 3

SHOW YOURSELF
A MAN

The Search for Fulfillment

*When the time drew near for David to die, he gave a charge to Solomon
his son. "I am about to go the way of all the earth," he said. "So be
strong, show yourself a man. And observe what the Lord your God
requires: Walk in his ways, and keep His decrees and commands, His
laws and requirements, as written in the Law of Moses, so that you
may prosper in all you do and wherever you go, and that the Lord
may keep His promise to me: 'If your descendants watch how they
live, and if they walk faithfully before me with all their heart and
soul, you will never fail to have a man on the throne of Israel.'"*

—1 Kings 2:1–4

very father wants his son to be strong and brave. This is another
way of saying "show yourself a man." But the question must be
asked: Is being brave and strong all that is required to demonstrate manhood? It would appear, according to today's definition
of manhood, that this would be enough. Yet there are many young men

alive today who are pursuing this perception of manhood and yet still are not fulfilled. Every man is seeking fulfillment. This implies that he is searching for a purpose that is larger than just his life. There must be a reason for being that is greater than self. Most young men have been taught that this involves preparing oneself to be responsible for a family. This is a very real part of each man's purpose, but a man's destiny lies beyond even his life as a father and a husband.

There is a biblical principle that must be observed here. This principle has to do with the male's understanding of manhood. Adam was given the responsibility to preserve order in the Garden of Eden. *The Lord made a garden in a place called Eden, which was in the east, and He put the man there* (Genesis 2:8). Notice that Eden was a chosen place where the Lord put Adam. Out of all the places available in the created world, this garden was specifically designed for the man. God has something definite in mind concerning the man. It must also be noted that only the man was physically in the earth at this time, the point being that whatever the Father designated for him to do was an indicator of the male's purpose. God revealed to Adam his role and responsibility at this time.

> *The Lord God took the man and put him in the Garden of Eden to work it and take care of it. And the Lord God commanded the man, "You are free to eat from any tree in the garden; but you must not eat from the tree of the knowledge of good and evil, for when you eat of it you will surely die."*
> —Genesis 2:1–17

The Father not only gave man purpose (to take care of the garden and look after it), but He also gave him responsibility. He was told that he had limitations. He had abundant freedom in that he could eat of all the trees in the garden. However, there was one tree from which he was not supposed to eat. One discovers that this mandate for Adam was greater than his own personal response. This lesson had to be learned and mastered by Adam because he would one day be responsible for communicating God's will to another human being. One of the greatest sources of fulfillment a man can experience is to successfully impart to his family the will of his heavenly Father. Hindsight reveals this was a real struggle for Adam, regardless of the reason Eve failed to observe this mandate. The Bible discloses that she was deceived by the serpent. However, be reminded that Adam was responsible not only to ensure she understood the will of the Father but also to provide a covering for her from the enemy. For the first time in their experience, something was desperately out of order. Eve had eaten from the tree of the knowledge of good and evil, but the shocking reality was nothing had changed. The Bible does not declare that her eyes were open or that she now knew something that her husband did not know. But in reality, there was now confusion in the Garden of Eden.

Adam was faced with this confusion. He was responsible for order in the garden. What did Adam do? *When the woman saw that the fruit of the tree was good for food and pleasant to the eye, and also desirable for gaining wisdom, she took some and ate it. She also gave some to her husband, who was with her, and he ate it. Then the eyes of both of them were opened, and they realized they were naked; so they sewed fig leaves together and made covering for themselves* (Genesis 3:6–7). For the very first time, Adam received something from Eve. To put it another way, the woman led the man, and the consequences were devastating. This point must not be misunderstood. It is a fact that God made man (mankind), male and female, and gave them the responsibility of dominion over all that He had created. In this sense, both the man and the woman are leaders.

However, the fall of mankind is not about leadership—it was obviously lacking. Rather, the fall was about order or, more specifically, the loss of it. When Adam took the fruit and ate it, everything changed. We are told that immediately the eyes of both of them were opened, and they realized they were naked. Everything changed, not because Eve was not a leader, but because Adam was responsible to lead and did not.

Adam and Eve confirmed this fact by hiding when they heard the Lord God walking in the garden. *But the Lord God called to the man, "Where are you?"* (Genesis 3:9). God called the man because he was responsible for the woman. Adam was accountable to God for both of their failures. A man's sense of fulfillment is connected to his ability to provide spiritual covering for his family, but God identifies the source of the problem. The woman truly had been deceived, but the man's disobedience was willful. *To Adam He said, "Because you listened to your wife and ate from the tree about which I commanded you, 'You must not eat of it,' Cursed is the ground because of you; through painful toil you will eat of it all the days of your life"* (Genesis 3:17). Adam chose to listen to the voice of his wife in spite of God's command. Confusion and disorder began with the man. If order is to be restored, it must also begin with the man. He is the one created by God to take care of and look after things. His absence or disobedience only perpetuates the increase of confusion and disorder in the earth.

With this in mind, one should better understand David's instructions to his son Solomon. David is talking about obedience on a kingdom level. He is imparting to his son not only the knowledge he needs but also a divine vision involving kingship over an eternal kingdom. It is imperative that Solomon grasps this vision for himself and for his seed's sake. David is near death but realizes this is the most important thing that he must do. The fulfillment of God's promise to him depends on it. His own personal sense of fulfillment is tied to it. Somehow Solomon must not fail. He must continue his father's vision and ensure that he shares the will of God with his sons so that God's promises come to pass. He must be aware that whatever he does will constitute change. He must comprehend that his failure will cause his children's eyes to be opened, and God will call for them.

The Manhood Mandate

David requested of his son one thing: "Show yourself a man." Whatever Solomon was to do to show himself a man was to be visible or observable. All too often men fail to realize that manhood is something that is visible. There are natural and spiritual markers identifying manhood. The word *show* is a military term. It means to "make a show of or to expose." It is best illustrated by Paul who wrote in Colossians 2:15: *And having disarmed the powers and authorities, He made a public spectacle of them, triumphing over them by the cross.* This verse demonstrates what God did through Christ. The Lord made a show of the enemy and exposed his defeat for the entire world to see. Jesus rose from the dead and proclaimed: "*. . . all authority in heaven and on earth has been given to me*" (Matthew 28:18). The unfortunate reality today is that men tend to think of themselves as the show. There is yet the tendency of men to become larger than life in their own eyes. The task before fathers is to help sons understand that their roles in life are truly ones of sacrifice. They will shine brightest by humbly leading their families according to the will of God.

When Paul wrote this verse, he was using a Roman military custom as a backdrop. When a Roman officer had won a major victory, it was customary for him to return to Rome in visible triumph. The victorious conqueror would enter the city at the head of a processional. He would hold up a trophy symbolizing his complete conquest of the enemy. He then was followed by his defeated enemy, often bound in chains, heads bowed, portraying their total submission to the conqueror. There was no escaping the shame and humiliation for the defeated enemy. Their disgrace was visible for all to see. This is the victory portrayed by Christ in His total defeat of Satan. *When he ascended on high he took many captives and gave gifts to his people. What does "he ascended" mean except that he also descended to the lower, earthly regions?* (Ephesians 4:8–9). Literally, Jesus defeated the enemy on his territory. He left no enemy alive. He recovered every soul from the bondage of hell and Satan!

In order to fully understand this victory, it must be realized that there is a battle between kingdoms. God is the Creator and owner of all things. *The earth and everything in it belongs to the Lord. The world and its people belong to Him* (Psalm 24:1). The Word verifies that the entire world and all its inhabitants belong to the Lord. Remember that when Adam and Eve sinned, everything changed. Sin was allowed to enter the world, and as a result, the world and its inhabitants came under a different influence. Before man sinned the world was under God's influence and man walked and talked with God. However, after man sinned his relationship with his Creator changed, and he was banished from the Garden of Eden. Romans 5:12 describes it this way: *Adam sinned, and that sin brought death into the world. Now everyone has sinned, and so everyone must die.* Before sin entered the earth, there was no death. Sin now represents the very nature of man. If a man is allowed to do whatever he desires without consequence, he most likely will sin. It is natural to him! It represents his nature or his tendency.

Sin also brought death. This meant that sin produced decay. Nothing will last forever. Be reminded again that David, too, is at the point of death, and be very certain death will happen to every living being. Death represents bondage—no man is exempt from it. Death does not represent the Father's will for man any more than sin represents His ways. In fact, God's will for man is that he would have a new nature. Jesus came into the world to save men from the destructive nature of sin and from its eternal consequences. The very first message that Jesus preached was: *Turn back to God! The Kingdom of Heaven will soon be here* (Matthew 4:17). This verse infers two things. First, sin is a reality in the earth, and men need to turn back to God. Next, it infers that Jesus comes to restore the Kingdom of God in the earth. If the Kingdom of God is to be restored in the earth, then the present kingdom must be overthrown. This simply means that sin and death must be defeated. Jesus overcame both sin and death through His resurrection. He died to save all men and rose from the grave proclaiming all power in heaven and in earth was restored to Him. Jesus, by His resurrection, made a show of the enemy, and now anyone who calls upon His name can be saved by faith.

The manhood mandate is a very serious call from God to men. Manhood is not achieved as a result of a biological clock. Neither is it obtained because a man is able to secure things for himself or his family. Rather, this mandate involves men being about the business of building the Kingdom of Heaven in the earth. It is about the restoration of the order of things according to the original plan of God. This mandate involves men because they were created with the divine purpose of taking care of and looking after things. Man must take his place and fulfill his purpose. This must be accomplished on every level. The male's responsibility is to watch over and guard his house, not allowing any enemy to come in and divide. Men must be strong and brave, but their battle is not a natural one. Men are called to expose the enemy wherever he may be found and to make a show of their triumph over him. This mandate must be passed from fathers to sons, from parents to children, from one generation to the next.

The Value of Vision
A Personal Testimony

Growing up as a preacher's kid, I often accompanied my father when he went to visit the sick. It is amazing the things you remember from the past and the effects they still have on you in the present. It seemed so obvious to me that people who were dying saw things that I could not see. What they saw was so clear to them, and most often what they shared in those moments represented their vision for their eternity. There were also times when we visited someone who knew that the end was near. They spoke words of faith and declared their readiness to meet the Lord. These were special times when a parent would entrust a word to a son, a daughter, or to the next generation. These often were their last words, and I had the opportunity to witness the comfort they gave to family members who were fortunate enough to hear them. They were words of vision that a loved one had for those being left behind.

King David saw something as he approached death. What he saw was clear to him, but it also meant the world to him. It was precious and dear to his soul. David saw something that was valuable and would prove profitable to Solomon if only Solomon could see it too. A man's vision should never die with him. David was successful because he was able to impart to his son Solomon the revelation of God's promise to him. Even though he was dying, he was imparting life. This moment was not just about him, nor was it about Solomon and his ascension to the throne. Rather, this moment was about God's vision revealed to David concerning His plan to restore His Kingdom in the earth. God had chosen Israel. He chose them so all the other nations would know there was a God in Israel.

God has always wanted His presence in the earth. Everything He created He called good. It was good because it fulfilled His purpose for creating it. God is glorified when the created thing fulfills His purpose for creating it. Man is the apex of God's creation and, as such, has a purpose to fulfill. Man was created to represent God's presence in the earth. Sin is the enemy's tool used to distract man so that he misses the purpose of God. Jesus revealed to His disciples the Father's plan in response to their request that He teach them how to pray:

> *You should pray like this:* "*Our Father in heaven, help us to honor your name. Come and set up your Kingdom, so that everyone on earth will obey you, as you are obeyed in heaven. Give us our food for today. Forgive us for doing wrong, as we forgive others. Keep us from being tempted and protect us from evil.*"
>
> —Matthew 6:9–13

Jesus reveals that in spite of the warfare that is raging, the Father's heart is for His Kingdom and reign to come in the earth. As a result of the restoration of His Kingdom, mankind would once again live according to His will. In essence, God wants His Kingdom in the earth just the way it is in heaven.

Every kingdom must have a king. The restoration of God's Kingdom in the earth requires having representation on the earth. This is the reason why God calls men. They are to represent His Kingdom in the earth. God laid the foundation for this revelation in Genesis in response to the snake for what he had done. God said: *"You and this woman will hate each other; your descendants and hers will always be enemies. One of hers will strike you on the head, and you will strike him on the heel"* (Genesis 3:15). As a result of this declaration, the war was on. From this point on, God was intent on finding a way to get His Kingdom in the earth.

History reveals that God called men and ultimately a nation. Yes, God chose Israel to be a unique nation unlike all the other nations. Israel was to represent the Lord's Kingdom in the earth. If God could hide His plan in a nation, He would be able to birth a king in the earth. It is no coincidence that the people of Israel missed this revelation. They wanted a king like all the other nations had. They failed to realize they were rejecting the Lord as their king in the process. To be more specific, they missed the plan of God not only for them, but for all men. Israel wanted a temporary king to rule over them while God wanted His Kingdom in the earth and His King upon the throne for all times. David caught this vision. He understood the heart of God. David got into agreement with God's vision for his life, for Israel, and for all mankind.

> *Then King David went in and sat before the Lord, and he said: "Who am I, O Lord God, and what is my family that you have brought me this far? And as if this were not enough in your sight, O God, you have spoken about the future of the house of your servant. You have looked on me as though I were the most exalted of men, O Lord God. What more can David say to you for honoring your servant? For you know your servant, O Lord. For the sake of your servant and according to your will, you have done this great thing and made known all these great promises. There is no God but you, as we have heard with our own ears. And who is like your people Israel—the one nation on earth whose God went out to redeem a people for himself, and to make a name for yourself, and to perform*

great and awesome wonders by driving out nations from before your people, whom you redeemed from Egypt? You made your people Israel your very own forever, and you, O Lord, have become their God. And now, Lord, let the promise you have made concerning your servant and his house be established forever. Do as you promised, so that it will be established and that your name will be great forever. Then men will say, 'The Lord Almighty, the God over Israel, is Israel's God!' And the house of your servant David will be established before you. You, my God, have revealed to your servant that you will build a house for him. So your servant has found courage to pray to you. O Lord, you are God! You have promised these good things to your servant. Now you have been pleased to bless the house of your servant, that it may continue forever in our sight; for you, O Lord, have blessed it, and it will be blessed forever."

—1 Chronicles 17:16–27

David believed God and was committed to His vision. Because David saw beyond the present, this vision became valuable. As a man, he may have missed the mark, but as a king, he walked with his God.

Missing What God Sees

There is a spiritual principle that must be learned in order to truly understand the ways of God. The Father rarely does things from a human perspective. Men often seem confused that God does things His way and not as men expect. This is why faith is required. Because Saul had become big in his own eyes and failed to obey the Lord's command, God rejected him as king over His people, Israel. *The Lord said to Samuel, "How long will you mourn for Saul, since I have rejected him as king over Israel. Fill your horn with oil and be on your way; I am sending you to Jesse of Bethlehem. I have chosen one of his sons to be king"* (1 Samuel 16:1). A discussion takes place between God and the prophet Samuel. The Lord not only shares with Samuel His regret of making Saul king, but also His solution to the problem. He directs Samuel to go to the house of Jesse, and there he will find a man that He has chosen.

God also had chosen Saul. But the Lord chose Saul at the request of the leaders of Israel. This represented the first process when Samuel was commanded to anoint a king. Samuel was told by God that He would send a man to him from the tribe of Benjamin who would rescue Israel from the oppression of the Philistines. For some reason outward features are emphasized. *Kish had a son named Saul, who was better looking and more than a head taller than anyone else in all Israel* (1 Samuel 10:2). After Samuel had met Saul, he anointed him with oil and informed him that the Lord had chosen him to be leader and ruler over His people. Samuel went through the process of calling each tribe until Saul was chosen. But when the time came to present Saul as king to Israel, he could not be found. Samuel had requested representation from each tribe to come to Mizpah to witness the proclamation of their new king. After praying, it was revealed that Saul was present but hiding. *They ran and brought him out, and as he stood among the people he was a head taller than any of the others. Samuel said to all the people, "Do you see the man the Lord has chosen? There is no one like him among all the people." Then the people shouted, "Long live the king!"* (1 Samuel 10:23–25).

It is apparent that Saul stood out from everyone else because of his appearance and his size. He seemed the perfect leader. He met all the required qualifications from man's perspective. Based on his outward appearance, he surely was the man for Israel. But the greater question must also be raised: Was he the man for God? Men, and especially women, have to be careful today because such priority is placed on appearance. People spend so much time making sure their appearance is acceptable or that it meets perceived expectations. In contrast, little if any, attention is placed on the inward person. Who is this person behind closed doors? What are his core values and what does he really believe? So many times individuals are accepted simply because they look the part, only to find out they lack the character to get the job done. Men must be keenly suspicious of the appearance game because it is used by the enemy to fuel false perceptions about manhood. In essence, a man can look the part and even play the role but this does not make him a man. Samuel was not exempt from these influences. He believed in Saul and was most likely influenced by his appearance as well. It was Samuel who mourned for Saul even after he was rejected by the Lord.

Samuel is told to go to Bethlehem to the house of Jesse. There he is to anoint one of Jesse's sons as the next king of Israel. Samuel is concerned that Saul might become aware of his intentions and kill him, but the Lord provides him with the proper covering he needs. A quick summation of what takes place is necessary. Samuel invited Jesse and his sons to participate in the sacrifice offered to the Lord. When Jesse and his sons arrived, the first thing Samuel noticed about his oldest son, Eliab, was his appearance. He was tall and handsome, and Samuel thought surely he was the one. But Samuel also must learn the lesson from which every human being would benefit. *But the Lord said to Samuel, "Do not consider his appearance or his height, for I have rejected him. The Lord does not look at the things man looks at. Man looks at the outward appearance, but the Lord looks at the heart"* (1 Samuel 16:7). Men must be discerning about the spirits of one another. This is a lesson for every person. One cannot be taken by appearance or distracted by outward beauty. The Lord reveals the plight of most people. They judge others based upon what they look like, but God judges everyone based upon what is in their hearts.

When Jesse ran out of sons who had appeared before Samuel, the Prophet inquired of Jesse: *"Are these all the sons you have?"* (1 Samuel 16:11). The answer was no, and David, who was taking care of the sheep, was sent for. Upon his arrival, the Lord confirmed that he was the chosen one. Note also that something is said about David's appearance. *So he sent and had him brought in. He was ruddy, with a fine appearance and handsome features* (1 Samuel 16:12). The appearance of Saul, the sons of Jesse, and even David serve as a reminder that God is not moved by the outward features of an individual. God is moved by the character and the commitment of one to His will. God is always captured by the man who makes His Word his priority, hiding it in his heart that he might remain upright before the Lord.

Although David was distracted by many things he saw in life, he was always committed to the Father's vision. As king, he remained focused on Kingdom business. He understood God's greater purpose and fought with all his heart to see the Father's will come to pass. He had comprehended the value of God's vision and was committed to see that his son understood it as well. King David's commitment to God's vision is best told by the apostle Paul.

> *Standing up, Paul motioned with his hand and said: "Men of Israel and you Gentiles who worship God, listen to me! The God of the people of Israel chose our fathers; he made the people prosper during their stay in Egypt, with mighty power he led them out of that country, he endured their conduct for about forty years in the desert. He overthrew seven nations in Canaan and gave their land to his people as their inheritance. All this took about 450 years. After this,*

God gave them judges until the time of Samuel the prophet. Then the people asked for a king and he gave them Saul son of Kish, of the tribe of Benjamin, who ruled forty years. After removing Saul, he made David their king. He testified concerning him: 'I have found David son of Jesse a man after my own heart; he will do everything I want him to do.'"

—Acts 13:16–23

Without a Vision the People Perish

Every man will be challenged in this life. It is clear that living in this world exposes mankind to the ills of sin. The spirit of this world leads men in a direction contrary to the Kingdom of God. The point cannot be emphasized enough concerning how the heavenly Father sees things. Because of the influence of this world, men have been conditioned to see things according to the outward appearance. Men are prone to agree with the models of this world. Even our youth gravitate to role models that reflect the spirit and image of this world. These models often include professional athletes, musicians, or others whose fame is the result of entertainment or some other highly visible medium. The spirit of this world promotes creature worship and births idolatry among this present generation. This self-identity is really conformity. The world continues to define life for men. Its vision of life is materialistic and self-serving. Life, according to the natural world, is about self-satisfaction. Man becomes the center of his own universe.

It is easy to become caught up in the ways of this world. This not only refers to the outward manifestations of one's actions or lifestyle, but also addresses the mentality of this world. In other words, the world wants mankind to think a certain way. Paul warned against this tendency while addressing the believers at Rome. *"Therefore, I urge you, brothers, in view of God's mercy, to offer your bodies as living sacrifices, holy and pleasing to God—this is your spiritual act of worship. Do not conform any longer to the pattern of this world, but be transformed by the renewing of your mind. Then you will be able to test and approve what God's will is—his good, pleasing and perfect will"* (Romans 12:1–2).

It is definitely implied that the goal of the world is to conform all men into a pattern that will reflect its spirit. The world is intentional in shaping the way men think. It wants men to think the way it thinks. As a result of this kind of thinking, men will miss God. They will not be able to comprehend the greater reason that reveals God's purpose for creating them. Literally speaking, the world wants men to walk in darkness. This is not a reference to sin in the sense of action, something you do, or something you have done. Rather, this is a reference to the attempt of the enemy to program your thinking. Commercialism is an example of the world driving patterns of thought through this vehicle. The calendar is used extensively, and every holiday becomes a tool by which the mentalities of all individuals are bombarded. This is the heart of commercialism, but it is also a reflection of the spirit of this world. Through commercialism man is perpetually influenced to continue living life from a materialistic and self-centered perspective. Children are taught at an early age that "things" are most important. Many adults define their identity and importance based upon the physical possessions they accumulate. For many people, this has become a way of life. For them, life is about accumulating more and more things of which they already have enough.

In contrast, the Father's desire is that men would be renewed in their thinking. The Lord desires that men's eyes would be opened, allowing them to see beyond the ploys of the enemy while avoiding the pitfalls that accompany it. The Father's desire is that all mankind would be transformed. This can only happen as a result of one's mind being renewed resulting in a transformed life. In other words, man would see differently. He would not become a slave to the present moment, but live life from an eternal perspective. Man would realize that although he has needs in this life, he was never created to live from a self-absorbed perspective. Men must comprehend that they are stewards of what has been entrusted to them. No man can be successful, able to test and approve what God's will is, if he is bigger than life in his own eyes.

This is why vision is absolutely necessary. Men especially must be able to see beyond themselves. David understood this principle. He recognized that God wanted him to be blessed, but he also realized that he was not to be bound by his blessings. David got it. He understood his presence in this world was temporary and that the greater purpose for which he had been born was to live on in others even after his death. When men break free from the darkness and deception of this world, they will again pursue their roles of authority, their places of leadership, and become the visionaries they were destined to be. Then the hearts of men will be turned towards their children because there is a vision in the man that must be revealed to his children. Fathers must realize the greater vision for their sons is that they become men who understand manhood in the light of God's Word and ordained purpose.

Men are faced with a generation following them who have no awareness of the old landmarks that confirmed manhood. Many of these men suffer because they were never exposed to the true vision of a father. They had no one speaking truth into their experience and grew up making choices based upon the trends and fads of their day. Many of these men are living frustrated lives, confused about life in general and relationships in particular. If there was ever a time when a vision for manhood needed to be cast, that moment is now. Sons desperately need fathers. Women are passionately attempting to find real men to marry. Daughters, too, need the affirmation of a father who serves as an example of the kind of man who will be in her future. In short, everyone seems to be looking for a vision of a man.

God serves as the source of men's visions. God has revealed to man his purpose, his responsibility, and his identity. Each of these is uniquely important. Man's purpose is to govern and to ensure that he provides a covering over all he governs. His responsibility is to provide for all of his family's needs. Men must provide more than just "things." They must provide vision, direction, and guidance to those who are under their responsibility. Furthermore, they must nurture their families, freeing them from the confusion of this world while exposing them to the promises of their Creator and their roles in carrying out the vision being imparted to them. Men must remind their families that they see things differently. They must speak truth into the lives of their children, ensuring they realize that their identities come from God and fulfillment in life comes from their discovery of His purpose for creating them. Like David, fathers must remind their children of God's promises made to them. Children must know His promises are real, and though they may not have been realized in the lives of their parents, they can be realized in them. Therefore children, like Solomon, must receive and commit to God's mandate concerning their families. God wants to do things in families that will take multiple generations to accomplish. This is why vision is so critical. This is why the man must be at the forefront leading this charge!

Chapter 4

YOU NEED TO KNOW WHO'S WATCHING YOU

Understanding Spiritual Vision

Everyone has encountered the person who was right and everyone else was wrong. In similar fashion, there is always that one individual who fails to get it. Everyone else is laughing, but this person wants to know what's funny. Everybody else is in agreement, but this person wants to know what's going on. Then there is the one who fails to see it. Everyone else appears to be catching a glimpse of the big picture while this person misses it. Jesus called twelve men—disciples—to follow Him. His intention was simple. He wanted to teach them about the Kingdom of God. In the process, He would reveal Himself to them as the Son of God. His ultimate goal was to disciple them, preparing them to represent the Kingdom of Heaven in the earth as apostles. However, there was one who missed it. Judas Iscariot failed to see the big picture and ultimately betrayed Jesus for thirty pieces of silver.

When it comes to Kingdom matters, it is not always easy to see clearly. Jesus had a conversation with Nicodemus about his ability to see the

Kingdom of God. Jesus declared: *"I tell you the truth, no one can see the Kingdom of God unless he is born again"* (John 3:3). In other words, when one is born again, he receives new life. He becomes new! This means that he no longer lives life dependent on his natural senses. As a new creation, man sees differently. He uses different faculties for sight. Paul, writing to the believers at Ephesus, prayed this way: *"I pray also that the eyes of your heart may be enlightened in order that you may know the hope to which he has called you, the riches of his glorious inheritance in the saints"* (Ephesians 1:18). This verse reveals that an individual may see through the eyes of his heart as opposed to his natural eyes. The ability to comprehend the revelations of God requires spiritual insight. Man must see using his spirit as opposed to using his natural sight. This faith is absolutely necessary in order to please God. In fact, *believers are to walk by faith rather than sight* (1 Corinthians 5:7). An individual sees differently because his perspective has changed. One is able to see the world, life, and experiences through the eyes of faith. This leads to seeing the way the Father sees.

God understands the importance of faith and one's ability to see differently. God calls this vision. When one understands the ways of God, he realizes the Father speaks vision into reality using faith. For example, when God initiated the process of creation, He spoke into reality the vision on the inside of Himself. God spoke light into existence. Light was real because God is light. This means light existed in God. Therefore, light represents the vision inside of God that He spoke into existence by faith. In other words, God believed that what He spoke would come to pass. *And God said, let there be light, and there was light* (Genesis 1:3). In essence, this is how the heavenly Father operates. He knows what is on the inside of Him, what is in His own heart. Then He releases that vision by using the Word, and by faith His declaration comes to pass. This is called His will! God reveals His will by sharing His Word with man. His promises will come to pass, and men are meant to be witnesses of His faithfulness.

When Israel asked for a king like all the other nations, this was contrary to the heart of God. Because it did not represent His heart, it also did not represent His will. Even though the leadership of Israel could not see this, Samuel the prophet saw it immediately. He was grieved in his own heart because he understood the heart of God. Thus he concluded that the people had rejected the Lord. God had chosen Israel to be His own people, and through their obedience He would be glorified. This would require faith and would demand that the people see His vision for them. The Bible reveals: *Where there is no revelation, the people cast off restraint; but blessed is he who keeps the law* (Proverbs 29:18). Where there is no vision, wherever the people are not able to see or comprehend the heart of the Father, they will miss His will for their lives. This was the sad reality that caused Samuel to be grieved. He realized that all of Israel had missed the heart of God. It is a blessing when men see the will of the Father for their lives. It is something worth celebrating when fathers discern God's greater purpose for their existence. God has a vision for every man, and it will require faith if that purpose is to be fulfilled in each life.

Israel missed the vision of God for them as a nation. They asked for a king, and God gave them Saul. The challenge God had was to reveal His vision to the king He had chosen. However, the greater challenge was for the king to see the heart of God and then, through obedience, allow God to fulfill His vision through him. What the people had missed, God, using the king, intended to reveal to them. The king would have to be able to see what the people could not see. The king would need to be able to comprehend what the people misunderstood. Saul would have to remain close to God if he was to see the bigger picture. This implies that God is seeking after men who are able to see the bigger picture. When a man fails to comprehend the heart of God, that man diminishes his ability to represent God. In fact, a man's failure to grasp the Father's greater vision could lead to his rejection by the Father.

Hindsight reveals that God was grieved that he had made Saul king. *Then the word of the Lord came to Samuel: I am grieved that I have made Saul King, because he has turned away from me and has not carried out my instructions* (1 Samuel 15:10–11). What caused the Father to come to this conclusion? The answer may be found in Samuel's response to Saul. *Samuel said, "Although you were once small in your own eyes, did you not become the head of the tribes of Israel? The Lord anointed you king over Israel"* (1 Samuel 15:17). There are a few revelations for every man in this response. First, when a man is small in his own eyes, he is able to see God's vision. When a man is humble and must be found in order to be presented to the people, he is in touch with the heart of the Father. Humility enables a man to walk with God. A second revelation is when a man is small in his own eyes, he has the potential to be elevated. It is a humble man that God seeks to exalt. This is the man God wants to use. This is a man with whom God can work.

Next, it must be acknowledged that Saul turned away from the Lord and failed to carry out His instructions. His turning away from the Father and his failure to obey the Lord both represent a process. This is not something that happened all at once. Samuel communicated to Saul that he was once small in his own eyes. The implication is obvious. Saul is no longer small in his own eyes, and the result of this is also predictable. When a man becomes exalted in his own eyes, his ability to see the bigger picture and God's greater purpose for his life is diminished. When a man becomes larger than life in his own eyes, his ability to fulfill the Father's will is compromised. Wives and children suffer as a result of this deception. The future is severely affected, even aborted in many cases, because of man's inability to follow instructions. The result is always confusion. Saul believed he had obeyed the Lord and had fulfilled divine purpose. However, the truth was he had misrepresented God before the people and failed to obey His will. As king, he was no different than the people he led. He totally missed God's heart and was blinded to His greater plan for His people in the earth. He could only see himself, and as a result, became part of the problem rather than the solution.

Notice that God never referred to Saul as a man after his own heart. This testimony is revealed only after Saul disobeyed. In other words, Saul is used as an example of a man who finds himself in a position contrary to the heart of God. Saul misinterpreted his own anointing. God did not call him to be The King, but only chose him as a king. As king, Saul was always meant to represent God the Father in the earth. His role was to lead the people to the revelation of the true King. God's intent concerning Saul was that he would catch a glimpse of the Kingdom. This Kingdom would have a King who would reign eternally. Saul's confusion became a distraction and nullified his ability to continue in the role of king. The Bible confirms this reality. *Because you have rejected the Word of the Lord, He has rejected you as king* (1 Samuel 15:23b).

Revelation Is Not Visible to Everyone

So he sent and had him brought in. He was ruddy, with a fine appearance and handsome features. Then the Lord said, "Rise and anoint him, he is the one." So Samuel took the horn of oil and anointed him

*in the presence of his brothers, and from that day on the Spirit of the
Lord came upon David in power. Samuel then went to Ramah.*
—1 Samuel 16:12–13

Revelation can be a tricky thing. One may not know when he is oper-
ating in it. In addition, those who hear it may not recognize it. Matthew 16
records a conversation between Jesus and His disciples. A brief summary
will reveal that Jesus asked His disciples the question: *"Who do the people
say that I am?"* (verse 13). They answer based on what they heard among
the people, declaring: *"Some say you are John the Baptist, others say Elijah,
and still others, Jeremiah or one of the prophets"* (verse 14). It is the tendency
of men to repeat what they have heard. The disciples were no different.
In other words, they were inclined to see things the way everyone else
saw them. This is a dangerous place for a man to be. For example, a man
cannot afford to always see things the way a woman sees them. He must
realize that he has a greater share of responsibility. Although the woman
shares responsibility with him, she is never responsible for him. The man
is always responsible for his wife and ultimately for his family. There may
be circumstances that reverse this order, but as a principle, it is accepted.
The man must see beyond himself. This may mean casting vision for his
family even when they don't agree with it.

Jesus became personal in His pursuit of an answer. Obviously their
response, simply echoing the thoughts of others, was not sufficient. Jesus
continued: *"But what about you?"* he asked. *"Who do you say that I am?"*
(verse 15). This is a reflective question that requires a little meditation. Jesus
is not just an ordinary man like everybody else. Jesus stands out. He stands
apart from the norm. In fact, He does things that ordinary men can't do.
He knows things that even educated men don't know. He is so different

that ordinary men want to know who His teacher was or from what school He graduated. The disciples had to be careful not to answer this question too quickly. Their answer must represent their perception of His true identity. Peter responded to the question as the outspoken and unconfirmed leader of the disciples. He declared: *"You are the Christ, the Son of the living God"* (verse 16). Jesus does not simply confirm that Peter's response was the right answer. Rather, Jesus announces the source of the answer. *"Blessed are you, Simon, son of Jonah, for this was not revealed to you by man, but by my Father in heaven"* (verse 17). What is Jesus really saying? He calls Peter blessed because Peter is able to see as He sees! Peter has connected with the Father. His eyes have been opened to see differently than everyone else around him. Even the other disciples had not seen what Peter saw. This is revelation! God wants men like Peter who are able to connect with His eternal plan. The Father seeks men who are able to see beyond the limits of the natural realm. God desires for men to walk in relationship with Him, to draw near to His throne so He can reveal His will to them. The ability to see Jesus is always bigger than the revelation itself.

Immediately after Jesus blessed Peter for his ability to see the Father's revelation, He continued to share with the disciples what would take place in the near future. Jesus shared revelation with all the disciples concerning the Father's purpose for them and the part they must play in the continued establishment of the Father's Kingdom on the earth.

> *"And I tell you that you are Peter, and on this rock I will build my church, and the gates of Hades will not overcome it. I will give you the keys of the kingdom of Heaven; whatever you bind on earth will be bound in heaven, and whatever you loose on earth will be loosed*

in heaven." Then He warned His disciples not to tell anyone that He was the Christ.

—MATTHEW 16:17–19

Be reminded that when Samuel anointed David, a number of things happened that were not visible to everyone present. First, when David arrived, the Lord spoke to Samuel revealing that he was the chosen one. It does not appear that God spoke His declaration in an audible voice that everyone present could hear. Samuel had come in peace to offer a sacrifice to the Lord and had invited Jesse and his sons to the sacrifice. As Jesse and his sons arrived, Samuel looked at each son and thought he was the chosen one beginning with the oldest son, Eliab. Even Samuel the prophet did not see as God did but saw based upon the outward appearance and visible qualities. However, he quickly discovered this was not the way the Father sees. God was looking for something greater and something deeper than the norm. The leadership of Israel had come requesting the status quo and desiring more of the same. Only Samuel knew the true purpose for his coming to Bethlehem. It is evident that Samuel wanted his purpose kept secret lest King Saul discover his plan and kill him. It is possible that even Jesse and his sons did not see what was really taking place before their very eyes? Is it possible even after Samuel took the horn of oil and anointed David in the presence of his family that not one of them saw David as a king?

Next it is revealed that once David had been anointed, from that day on the Spirit of the Lord came upon him. This, too, was not visible to his family. There appears to be no noticeable sign of change. David did not do anything different in that moment, although everything changed from that moment on. It takes an anointing from the Lord in order to rule over Israel, but it must also be realized that he was anointed as a husband and as a father. Regardless of his role, each man needs God's anointing if he is to be successful. The anointing opens the eyes of a man, enabling him to see himself as a representative of a greater kingdom.

Missing Revelation

When does a man recognize the king in himself? Meditate on the following revelation:

> In every man there is a king.
> It would be a shame to live your life and never reign.
> And though your kingship will always be challenged,
> Never settle for the man and miss the king!

Recognizing the king inside each man requires the anointing. God the Father must reveal to each man the process that leads to that moment when he discovers the king inside of himself. The king has always been there, but there are ordained moments when he must emerge. If each man is to recognize his authority, it must always be as a result of respecting God's Spirit. Remember that at the time David was anointed, the Spirit of the Lord came upon him. God's Spirit always brings power. It is the Holy Spirit that empowers and enables a man to see and energizes the being of a man, exposing him to his original calling and reminding him of his position of dominion. When men are anointed and touched by God's power, something changes in them. For the first time, their eyes are opened to the possibility that they were never created to settle only for the man who is limited by his nature. As a result of this revelation, they are free to pursue the king.

When Samuel anointed David, it is possible that God revealed Himself in a personal and tangible way. David was ushered into the very presence of God. Being in God's presence will change any man's life. David later testified of this reality. *You have made known to me the path of life; you will fill me with joy in your presence, with eternal pleasures at your right hand* (Psalm 16:11). A second version reads this way: *Thou wilt show me the path of life: in thy presence is fullness of joy; at thy right hand there are pleasures for evermore* (KJV). God's presence has the power to transform lives. Moses was not the same man after he encountered God's presence through a burning bush. It was there on holy ground that Moses saw with his own eyes the glory of the Lord. On the mountain called Horeb he heard the voice of the Lord revealing to him the Father's divine purpose for His people. In Acts, Luke recorded Saul's unexpected meeting with the Lord on the road to Damascus. There he experienced the presence of the Lord described as a light from heaven that shined so brightly that Saul was struck blind. Yet in this moment he heard a voice from heaven convicting him of his confusion while delivering him from deception. It only took a moment for Saul's life to be completely rewritten. He was Saul the persecutor when he began his journey to Damascus, but he was Paul the apostle when he arrived there. He received his calling in the presence of the Lord. *But the Lord said to Ananias, "Go! This man is my chosen instrument to carry my name before the Gentiles and their kings and before the people of Israel"* (Acts 9:15).

Like Moses on the mountain of God, David, after being anointed, received a revelation of God's heart for His people. Just as Paul's eyes were opened to see the greater purpose for his life, now David began to see the possibilities in store for him. The anointing does remove burdens and destroys yokes, but it also can awaken a man from spiritual slumber.

No doubt, David had become content with his place as the baby son and had convinced himself that he would never surpass his brothers or ever live up to his father's expectations. He probably had resigned himself to the simple task of caring for the sheep. Is it possible that David had missed God's revelation about himself as well? This happens far too often! Men believe what others tell them about themselves. They simply submit to the image of themselves portrayed by those around them. How many men have become the pictures painted by their wives? How many men have never gone beyond the image of a baby perpetrated by their mothers? God is determined that men would see themselves as He sees them. God sees the king in men!

Something happened to David when he was anointed. Something changed in his vision and his heart that he was not fully able to comprehend. He knew without knowing that he was not the same man. Every man must realize those divine moments and appointed times when something clicks on the inside of him. In those special times, he realizes things he didn't know before or things he never really understood. In those moments his eyes are opened, and he is able to see beyond himself. For the first time, he realizes the leader he really is. He is awakened to his true potential and becomes excited about his responsibility. He begins to ponder the possibilities now available to him but now sees himself in the lead. In short, he has begun his pursuit of the king!

David returned to taking care of the sheep, but things were different now because of the anointing. As a result, he was able to understand the things happening to him in light of God's greater plan and began to look at things from the Father's perspective. He was more discerning than he had ever been before. Now everything had to be interpreted through the revelation of God's Word revealed by Samuel. He realized that there was a king inside of him. His future and his destiny had changed. He was now on a different path than before and knew that his identity had changed. He was now aware that someone else was directing his future. Even though Jesse was his earthly father, he was no longer in charge of his future. Whatever his plans might have been for David, they had been usurped by God's greater plan. No doubt his brothers would have always wanted him to be subject to them, but suddenly they had lost their ability to control him. David was different! For the first time in his life, he would understand why God allowed both a lion and a bear to attack his sheep. He responded differently because now he was a king.

Everything happens by process. Having been anointed to be a king did not make David the king in that very moment. The experiences that happened to a shepherd boy would later be interpreted by a king. When the lion and bear attacked the sheep, David could only interpret this experience through the eyes of a shepherd boy. His earthly father had given him the task of watching over the sheep. They were his responsibility and he had to learn what this meant while gaining respect for his father's house. He represented his father while caring for the sheep, and he had to realize he was a part of his father's vision. Regardless of how big or small his task, he needed to learn faithfulness. He could not spend his time pouting about his job in comparison to his brothers. Rather, he learned to be focused and determined to finish the task assigned to him. After all, the sheep were dependent on him. Herein lies a great revelation. The anointing of God takes one's eyes off the task and focuses them on those for whom the task is required. The fact is the sheep needed a shepherd!

The Transfer of Vision—The Process

Life is full of transitions, and every man must respect this reality. One must transition from immaturity to maturity, from dependency to independence. Men must transition from being unemployed to being employed. They must move from follower to leader, from being provided for to becoming the provider. They also must transition in their character. They must leave disobedience for obedience, undisciplined for discipline, and unfaithfulness for trustworthiness. They must transcend the present for the future. No one can achieve these realities without enduring the process. There are lessons to learn that can only be learned as a result of the process. If one is not careful, he will interpret his experiences independent of the process. This is the reason why so many experiences are misunderstood. Jesus serves as a supreme example of the process. There were many experiences that His disciples misunderstood simply because they were not aware of the process. Many times Jesus assured the disciples that certain things had to happen. Of course He was aware of the process. He understood the end from the beginning. Jesus lived His life focused on the end and therefore interpreted every experience from that perspective. One thing that stands out about Jesus was His obedience and commitment to the process. This is why He is the best example for men. *Let us fix our eyes on Jesus, the author and perfecter of our faith, who for the joy set before Him endured the cross, scorning its shame, and set down at the right hand of the throne of God* (Hebrews 12:2).

Men struggle with faith because they do not know the end from the beginning. This is why faith requires obedience. God reveals His promises to men, and those promises become their purpose. This is what God did with David. He promised David that his seed would always be represented on the throne of Israel. Furthermore he was promised that from his seed a king would come whose reign would never end. This would be an eternal kingdom. David must realize this was much bigger than he himself. His priority must be the Father's priority. Regardless of the distractions along the way, in spite of his personal failures, he must remain faithful to the heavenly vision. Put another way, he must not lose sight of the promises of God.

What does the process look like? Two verses bring clarity to understanding the answer. *So Samuel took the horn of oil and anointed him in the presence of his brothers, and from that day on the Spirit of the LORD came powerfully upon David. Samuel then went to Ramah. Now the Spirit of the LORD had departed from Saul, and an evil spirit from the LORD tormented him* (1 Samuel 16:13–14). It is worth noting that one verse follows the other, the point being that at the same time the Spirit of the Lord came upon David, it also departed from Saul. Could this mean that God never anoints two men for the same task at the same time? Saul was the king. The emphasis must be on the verb *was*. Even though he was still the king, he was no longer anointed for the position. Men must be careful about remaining in positions or places without the anointing. Saul's intent to kill David was public knowledge. Saul seemed to think by killing David he might regain the anointing. But it was his disobedience that had caused him to lose favor with God. Killing David would not restore Saul to the throne. Although Saul was still king, the deeper problem was that he had lost sight of the king in himself.

On the other hand, David now found himself under the mantle of kingship and had to discover the king in himself. This discovery would require a process. The Bible reminds us: *And we know that in all things God works for the good of those who love him, who have been called according to his purpose* (Romans 8:28). This verse implies that God is also at work to see that His purposes prevail. The Lord is simply looking for men He can use. In order for God to use a man, he must first be yielded and moldable. The Father must prepare the man for the task he has been called to perform. David was beginning the process of preparation. David's preparation begins with Saul's torment. One man has lost the anointing while another man has received it. In response to Saul's torment, his servants were commanded to search for someone who played the harp. It was hoped that this would bring comfort to the king. As it would happen, one of the servants just happened to know about David's gift in playing the harp. Saul sent a messenger to Jesse with this request: *Send me your son David, who is with the sheep* (1 Samuel 16:19). God used David's gift to bring him into the presence of the king. Remember, David has been anointed to become king. What better way to learn about kingship than to learn from the king himself. It is amazing how God works things together to accomplish His purpose. David was a blessing to King Saul. *David came to Saul and entered his service. Saul liked him very much, and David became one of his armor-bearers. Then Saul sent word to Jesse, saying, "Allow David to remain in my service, for I am pleased with him"* (1 Samuel 16:21–22). Literally speaking, Saul loved David. He was pleased with him and desired for him to remain in his service. David was now one of those in the inner circle of the king. David's gift had made room for him, but God was also positioning David in order that he might elevate him.

When God uses someone, He moves them from one place to another, from one position to another, and from one level to another level. David, the youngest of his brothers, had moved from shepherding sheep to being anointed as king. He had moved from his father's house to serving in the king's house. Furthermore, he was about to be moved from the level of being unknown to a level of notoriety fit only for a king. When God wants to use someone, He elevates that person in the eyes of others. Everyone begins to see that individual the way God sees him. David was now an armor-bearer for King Saul. In this position of service, he had access to the king, yet he was only noticed by those close to the king as well as members of the king's household. He was traveling back and forth from his father's home where he served as shepherd over his father's sheep to the house of the king where he brought comfort and peace to the leader of Israel. During that time the Philistine army had declared war on Israel and had gathered their army at Socoh in Judah. Their champion, Goliath, had made a habit of challenging the army of Israel, by inviting one man to fight him. Whoever won that battle would in essence be the victor between the two nations. The Philistines put their hope in their champion, but who did the Israelites put their trust in? History records the fact that King Saul was well advanced in years. The assumption would be that he was not able to stand against the giant. As a result, he had promised great wealth to the man who would defeat Goliath. In addition, he promised to give his daughter in marriage to the victor and to exempt this warrior's family from paying taxes in Israel.

David's older brothers had joined King Saul's army and had gone off to battle. As usual, David remained home with his father. But Jesse became concerned for his sons and sent David with provisions for them. It is probable that this was not the first time this happened. It is also possible that this trip was one of providence. It is part of the process that God used to elevate David in the eyes of Israel. *Early in the morning David left the flock in the care of a shepherd, loaded up and set out, as Jesse had directed. He reached the camp as the army was going out to its battle positions, shouting the war cry* (1 Samuel 17:20). The point is made that both armies positioned themselves for battle. As was his custom, Goliath stepped forward and proclaimed his usual defiance. In similar fashion, the men of Israel did what they were accustomed to doing—retreating from him in great fear.

This represents many men today. Like Israel, men are dressed up for battle, but are not ready to fight! The Bible reveals that Goliath had defied Israel for forty days, and no man in Israel had responded to his challenge. Is it possible for men to be in position but lack the anointing to respond to the challenges of their day? There are many men who are in the position of a father but have failed to fulfill the calling of fatherhood. There are men in the position of a brother but have failed to sharpen their brothers. There are men in the position of husbands but have failed to move, to cover their wives and families. There are scores of men who are dressed up for battle but not ready to fight.

In contrast, David had a different spirit. David had been anointed, and from that moment on he saw things differently. God wills that men would walk under the anointing of the Holy Spirit guided by its power. David demanded answers to two questions. *What will be done for the man who kills this Philistine and removes this disgrace from Israel? Who is this uncircumcised Philistine that he should defy the armies of the living God?* (1 Samuel 17:26). When the Spirit of the Lord is upon a man, two things will happen. First, he will not be content until everything bringing disgrace upon his heavenly Father is destroyed. Next, he will identify and stand against every enemy who would threaten his home and family. David was brought before King Saul, and the king even tried to give him his armor to wear. David declared he could not enter battle with armor that had not been proven. This is a very real concept. Men should never enter battle with someone else's armor, especially armor that has not been proven. In other words, what works for one man may not work for another man. Each man should have his own armor and should know what works for him. Like David, each man should be able to testify concerning his armor having been tested, and more importantly, proven.

David killed the giant, and then the men of Israel engaged in battle. *When the Philistines saw that their hero was dead, they turned and ran. Then the men of Israel and Judah surged forward with a shout and pursued the Philistines to the entrance of Gath and to the gates of Ekron. Their dead were strewn along the Shaaraim road to Gath and Ekron* (1 Samuel 17:51b–52). It was only after Goliath was slain that the men of Israel moved forward in battle. These men can be referred to as "then men." They will never enter the battle until someone else has already defeated the enemy. "Then men" are dependent on someone else to lead. Even though Saul was old and could not fight himself, there should have been men under his leadership who would represent him in battle.

What happens to families when there are no men to fight for them? How will the next generation of sons know how to fight if the men of this generation only stand on the sidelines and never enter the battle? God is looking for men who have the spirit of David on their lives. These are men who will step forward when no one else will. It can be dangerous to be this kind of man because this man brings attention to himself and becomes a threat to every other man. Consider the following insight:

> *As Saul watched David going out to meet the Philistine, he said to Abner, commander of the army, "Abner, whose son is that young man?" Abner replied, "As surely as you live, Your Majesty, I don't know." The King said, "Find out whose son this young man is."*
> —1 Samuel 17:55–56

Chapter 5

THE LEADERSHIP GAP

The Source of Leadership

eadership comes from God. It is who He is. In other words, God is always a leader, and He is *the* leader. There is never a leadership gap with the Lord. Why is this true? It is true simply because God leads from eternity. This is why God can say something in the Old Testament promising a seed to be born and conclude in the New Testament that in the fullness of time a baby is born. No one is more focused than the Father. No one is more intentional, more purposeful than God. It takes leadership to run a universe, to operate a world, and to be mindful of every created thing. There can be no gaps in leadership with this much at stake. The word *gap* is defined two ways. First, it is simply defined as an opening. When there is an opening, it allows things or people to enter or exit. In spite of the intention, when there is an opening, one does not have complete control. Access can be gained illegally simply because of the opening. Next, the word *gap* is defined as an empty space. This implies lack or that something is missing. The Bible reminds mankind: *In the beginning God created the heavens and the earth. Now the earth was formless and empty, darkness was over the surface of the deep, and the Spirit of God was hovering over the waters* (Genesis 1:1–2). God is never content with empty spaces, especially those covered by darkness.

Wherever there is a gap in authentic leadership, the results are always the same. The absence of leadership allows for openings and causes those covered by the leader to become exposed. Furthermore, when there is a leadership gap, it creates a vacuum that demands a leader, but one cannot always be found. In most cases these gaps are the result of leaders with temporary vision who are unable or unwilling to see beyond themselves. Saul serves as an example of this kind of a leader. He was unable to lead beyond the temporary. Because of his inability, he failed to please God and was ultimately rejected by God. However, he was aware that something had changed. He had lost the anointing. He had been told in no uncertain terms that God was not pleased with him. *As Samuel turned to leave, Saul caught hold of the hem of his robe, and it tore. Samuel said to him, "The Lord has torn the kingdom of Israel from you today and has given it to one of your neighbors—to one better than you. He who is the Glory of Israel does not lie or change His mind; for He is not a man that He should change His mind"* (1 Samuel 15:27–29). The leaders of Israel asked God for a king because they were experiencing a leadership gap, and God chose Saul. This leadership gap allowed the enemy to distract them from God's eternal plan to one that was merely temporary. In essence, they rejected God as their eternal king and wanted a temporary king like all the other nations. As a result, Saul was chosen as their first king.

Saul the man had to then become Saul the king. Notice at the beginning Saul was intimidated by this proposition. When it was time to introduce him as king, he was hiding. Samuel the prophet affirmed this reality by reminding Saul: *"Although you were once small in your own eyes, did you not become the head of the tribes of Israel?"* (1 Samuel 15:17). This reminder came after Saul had disregarded the commandment of the Lord. Every man, including Saul, must avoid the pitfall of becoming too big in his own eyes. Each man must realize it is God's anointing on his life that permits him to fulfill the role he was created to perform. Men must be reminded that whatever they have achieved is by God's grace, not because of title or position. It is the Lord who exalts the humble, but those filled with pride are destined for a fall. When men become prideful and big in their own eyes, this creates a leadership gap. Men have a very real role to play in this life, but because of pride, gaps have manifested, exposing wives and children to deception and darkness. Like the sons of Samuel, generations of youth have been distracted by the cares of this world and have been caught up in a temporary perception of life. They have lost sight of the true King and His purpose for their lives. Fathers must take the lead in representing God's leadership in the earth, reminding those they cover of the true Leader. This is the role of the man.

The man is the glory of God. He is to be a witness of leadership in the earth pointing others to the heavenly Father. The man is responsible to lead, and this is his created purpose. The enemy desires to ambush entire generations and lead them astray. By using the things of this world, he wills to distract them from their divine purpose. The things of this world represent empty space. Regardless of how much value one may give them, they are only temporary and do not possess the ability to truly fulfill. This is why generations must be taught that life is more than food and drink. There is more to life than what one will wear. God is looking for men who will live right and promote truth. He is seeking men who have a heart after His. These are men who truly know Him and are committed to His plan above their own. These are men who have an eternal perspective because they have seen a heavenly vision and God has dealt with the gaps in their minds. They recognize God as their leader and will not only follow Him, but are also determined to lead others to Him. Paul the apostle is a fitting example of this truth. Toward the end of his life, he testified that he was completely changed. He made a most concise statement while testifying before King Agrippa. *"I was not disobedient to the vision from heaven"* (Acts 26:19). Paul had seen the light and then was able to see from God's perspective. When God reveals Himself to men, it changes the way they see. Men must realize the vision that God has for their lives and then entrust that vision to their sons.

Seeing an Anointed King

It has already been established that not everyone can see from an eternal perspective. In other words, not every man can see what the Father sees. Men must grasp the vision and heart of God if they are to see as the Father sees. The man to whom God revealed His plan must realize the Father's plan may not be fulfilled in his lifetime. David received the promise of God knowing he would be a part of an eternal kingdom established in the earth. He realized he was part of a revelation that was ahead of its time. God made a promise to redeem mankind and restore man once again to his created position of dominion. The promise was solidified with Abraham who, as a result of faith, became the Father of many nations. God's plan required the involvement of multiple generations. But the plan of God to establish an eternal kingdom, one that would never end, required a king who would usher in the Father's will in the earth. David was chosen by God as king over Israel, and through his lineage would come the King of kings. David understood this promise and realized he must provide leadership without gaps.

The challenge with this revelation is that the present king did not see David the way God did. Furthermore, Saul had sons, and one of his sons would most likely succeed him. If God's purpose is to prevail in the earth, someone must receive a revelation from the Lord. It is true God does work His will in all things, but He uses people to accomplish this. A good example of this involved Jonathan, the son of Saul.

> *After David had finished talking with Saul, Jonathan became one in spirit with David, and he loved him as himself. From that day Saul kept David with him and did not let him return to his father's house. And Jonathan made a covenant with David because he loved him as himself. Jonathan took off the robe he was wearing and gave it to David, along with his tunic, and even his sword, his bow and his belt.*
> —1 SAMUEL 18:1–4

It is obvious Saul's perception of David changed. Saul had David brought to him after he had slain Goliath. King Saul had his eyes on David as he went out to meet the enemies of Israel. This may well be the moment when Saul began to get the revelation concerning David. In any case, David was no longer permitted to return home. He had to remain with the king. But Saul was not the only one who noticed a shifting in the atmosphere. David has risen to prominence in a very short period of time. He appeared on the scene relatively unknown. He drew the attention of those soldiers around him because of his questions but also because of his spirit. There was something different about him as a result of the anointing. God was with David, and His Spirit drove him. God's Spirit was grieved within him as he witnessed the challenge of the giant and no response from the men of Israel. It was the king inside of him that was burdened for a nation suffering from a leadership gap.

When the enemy camps at the front door of men's lives, God looks for a king who will go out and fight the enemy for His name's sake. Though all other men are gripped with fear, God looks for a king He can put in charge. Men will dress up for battle, but kings will actually fight. Wherever the king leads, men will follow. All of Israel was now aware of David. He had become a part of the nation's history. It is important that men are discerning of the challenges being faced as they begin their transformations to become kings. Every man must make this journey. The sad reality is far too many men return as the same man who left. Some men never discover the kings in themselves.

Jonathan was no exception. Obviously, he was not aware of what was happening in his midst. He was the king's son. There were demands placed on him and expectations that he had to meet. No doubt, Jonathan had wrested within himself because of his own lack of response to Goliath. There might have been the expectation that he would lead as the king's son. Potentially, questions were being raised as to the failure of Saul's sons to come forward. Leadership was not passed from Eli to his sons. Is it possible that this was happening again?

As a son, Jonathan was close to his father. Saul was already cautious of David and had made the decision to keep him close where he could see him. David no longer would be able to wonder off on his own to pursue his identity. He must remain under the watchful eye of the king. But how did Jonathan feel about all of this? Was he suspect of David now that he was popular? Was David a threat to his own future? What was going on in the mind of Jonathan? Who was David *really,* and where did he come from? What was he after? Was he pursuing the throne? By killing the Philistine giant, David was already the recipient of some noticeable exceptions to the life of the common citizen. David's family also became visible by association. Because of David, many things had changed. But Jonathan must have been aware of David even before his victory over Goliath. His father was sick and tormented, and David was the armor-bearer who played the harp to soothe his father's pain. In this role, David was no soldier. He was a shepherd boy with a gift that brought healing to his father. In short, Jonathan knew David.

It was after David had finished responding to King Saul's questions that something divine took place. Jonathan, the Bible says, became one in spirit with David and loved him as a brother. This kind of relationship demanded time and required opportunity to prove one's faithfulness. Perhaps Jonathan was moved over time by David's loyalty and faithfulness in serving his father. It is also possible that Jonathan was aware of how David had been treated by his own father. As Saul's perception and feelings about David changed, no one would know this better than Jonathan. This was not an easy task for David, and things were destined to only get worse. It may not be obvious why Jonathan loved David, but the fact is he did. It is important that men understand this. First, it speaks to the power of genuine brotherhood. Jonathan loved David as he loved himself. He apparently treated David well even though this seemed contrary to his position. David was seen as the enemy by many, including his father. To become a brother to David could jeopardize his future while compromising his inheritance. And yet it is revealed that Jonathan made a covenant with David.

Every man needs a real brother. These kinds of relationships seem to be dwindling. In generations past, these relationships were symbolized by fathers and sons, between brothers, and most often among classmates. These were friendships that would last for lifetimes. Today it is difficult at best to identify these kinds of relationships. So much has changed, and because so much of the focus is now on temporary things, men find themselves more isolated, concerned only for themselves. As a result, more and more young men are attempting to eliminate leadership gaps. Proverbs 27:17 declares, *As iron sharpens iron, so one man sharpens another.* This is what real brotherhood is all about. Men are to sharpen one another to ensure that the Father's will is fulfilled in every man's life. Remember, men receive their being and their purpose from the Lord. Leadership gaps exist when men fail to fulfill their God-ordained purpose and attempt to complete alone what was always ordained to be accomplished together. Men have always followed men, but God's will is that men would follow kings.

Jonathan could have limited his perception of David to the man. In this sense, he saw David as everyone else did. As a man, David was a threat to his future as the next king in Israel. As a man, Jonathan would be concerned about David's recognition and acceptance among the people. But Jonathan saw past the man and recognized a king. Is it possible that Jonathan was able to see what even David's own family missed? He was not present when Samuel anointed David to be the next king in Israel, but he nonetheless recognized the anointing on David's life. People, even other men, may not recognize the man you are, but they will respect the king in you. Jonathan recognized the anointed leader David was. He had witnessed this before when his father was anointed king. But he was now aware that something had changed. Even his own father had failed to discern the favor now on David.

Jonathan became one in spirit with David and loved him as a brother. As a result, Jonathan made a covenant with David. This was symbolized by his removal of his robe, his tunic, his sword, his bow, and even his belt.

In essence, he was submitting himself to David. This was no small act for Jonathan. He not only was submitting himself to David, but he was also submitting his right to the throne, his very future, to David. This is true brotherhood. When men are able and willing to submit all to another and trust they will be protected, true brotherhood has been established. This kind of brotherhood is seriously lacking today. Men don't know to whom they can entrust their very lives. They don't know where to go to find covering for their futures. Men need leaders they can stand under and brothers they can stand with. This represents a cry for a king!

The Elevation of a King

It is established that Saul's motives concerning David were suspect. Saul obviously saw David as a potential threat. He restricted David's freedom to his own home, no longer permitting him to leave. Unlike his son Jonathan, Saul was unable to submit to the anointing now on David's life. In part, he recognized that David was different. It was not just the fact that he had triumphed over Goliath, but more importantly, it was his spirit. David brought a fresh faith to the battlefield. God had proven Himself to David as a shepherd under attack by a lion and a bear. In both cases, the Lord had given David victory. No doubt these training opportunities were meant to teach David to depend on the Lord. David understood it was the Lord who caused him to triumph. David also possessed a keen awareness that he must fight with what had been proven. When he was brought before King Saul, the king attempted to send David against Goliath with his armor. However, David was a shepherd boy and not a soldier. He had no armor, at least by natural appearances. David knew that if he had experienced victory in the past, he could experience it again in the present. In short, it made no difference to David whether he faced a lion, a bear, or Goliath. He knew God would give him the victory.

Men must be careful because Satan will always attempt to use their enemies to deceive them. A bear and a lion may represent challenges men faced in the past, but those same men will have to face their Goliaths in the present. Apparently, all the men of Israel were paralyzed by the fact that Goliath was a giant, but David was not shaken! God gives men victory over their enemies, but sometimes men cannot see the enemy for the giant. This point was made unmistakably when the children of Israel arrived at the Promised Land. *The Lord said to Moses, "Send some men to explore the land of Canaan which I am giving to the Israelites"* (Numbers 13:1). God had promised the children of Israel a specific land prepared for them. He described the land as flowing with milk and honey. This excited the Israelites because they had been in bondage in Egypt and had now come through the desert. What they had been promised by the Word of the Lord was about to become a reality in their own experience. This is what faith really is all about! One must take God at His Word and trust Him until the promise is manifested in his experience.

Leaders from each of the tribes of Israel went into the land as spies to see if it was everything God said it was. Their responsibility was to return to the people and give a report concerning the land. They were to see what the land was like. They were to observe the inhabitants of the land and report whether they were strong or weak, whether the cities were walled or fortified, and whether the land was productive. Everything rested on the report of these men. Oftentimes leaders fail to realize the weight associated with leadership. In similar fashion, men don't always realize the enormous responsibility they have as husbands, fathers, providers, and protectors. So much is at stake, and much can be lost if leadership is misrepresented.

> *They came back to Moses and Aaron and the whole Israelite community at Kadesh in the Desert of Paran. There they reported to them and to the whole assembly and showed them the fruit of the land. They gave Moses this account: "We went into the land to which you sent us, and it does flow with milk and honey! Here is its fruit. But the people who live there are powerful, and the cities are fortified and very large. We even saw descendants of Anak there. The Amalekites live in the Negev; the Hittites, Jebusites and Amorites live in the hill country; and the Canaanites live near the sea and along the Jordan." Then Caleb silenced the people before Moses and said, "We should go up and take possession of the land, for we can certainly do it." But the men who had gone up with him said, "We can't attack those people; they are stronger than we are." And they spread among the Israelites a bad report about the land they had explored. They said, "The land we explored devours those living in it. All the people we saw there are of great size. We saw the Nephilim there (the Descendants of Anak come from the Nephilim). We seemed like grasshoppers in our own eyes, and we looked the same to them."*
> —NUMBERS 13:26–33

This created a leadership gap. Only two of the twelve leaders were able to keep their focus on the Lord and His promise rather than on the situation and circumstances. In contrast, the other ten leaders gave a bad report and influenced the people into rebelling against God. Of course, the end result of this rebellion caused an entire generation to miss the promise of God and to die in the wilderness. These leaders misrepresented the purpose of God. God had promised them the land. However, they forgot about the land and became consumed with the giants. They even perceived themselves as grasshoppers in light of the giants. Leadership gaps will always occur when men view themselves in light of their situation or enemy faced. Like the two men who did not waver in spite of the giants, men must remain committed to the promise of God. He has not changed His mind. From the Lord's perspective, if He promised the children of Israel the land, then the giants simply came with the land!

David became a witness for every man by responding as a king when challenged by the enemy. Jonathan observed David just as his father did. It is evident that the two men saw David differently. Saul restricted David's freedoms and began to make decisions concerning him with questionable motives. He attempted to involve David in war campaigns with the potential hope of his defeat or even his death. However, God was with David, and he found favor continuously in all that he undertook. This favor caused David to be elevated even by King Saul. *Whatever Saul sent him to do, David did it so successfully that Saul gave him a high rank in the army. This pleased all the people and Saul's officers as well* (1 Samuel 18:5). David continued to be elevated in the eyes of Israel. The people of Israel clearly saw David's leadership potential.

> *When the men were returning home after David had killed the Philistine, the women came out from all the towns of Israel to meet King Saul with singing and dancing, with joyful songs and with tambourines and lutes. As they danced, they sang: "Saul has slain his thousands, and David his ten thousands." Saul was very angry; this refrain galled him. "They have credited David with tens of thousands," he thought, "but me with thousands. What more can he get but the kingdom?" And from that time on Saul kept a jealous eye on David.*
>
> —1 Samuel 18:6–8

Saul clearly was aware of David's popularity among the people. He was threatened personally, but for all the wrong reasons. He was so focused on David's strengths and potential that he was blinded to his own weaknesses. In addition, he was aware he had lost favor with the Lord. He became angry and jealous in response to the people's description of David. Saul began to respond to his own fears. He viewed David as a threat to his hold on the kingdom. The reality was that the kingdom did not belong to him. Regardless of his insecurities, he could not control the people or their celebration of David. He was a jealous king who was blinded to God's greater plan and concluded that David was the problem.

In contrast, Jonathan loved David and saw him as a beloved brother. He pledged his loyalty to David and probably was one of the officers who was moved by David's successes. Jonathan saw the king in David. He may have been unsure about David's gifts, but he was convinced that those gifts had made room for him. What was happening in Israel could not be controlled or hindered by any man. This was a hard reality for Jonathan to accept because it magnified the strengths of David while exposing the weaknesses of his own father. Jonathan had to find the balance to deal with his father and David. The fact is that God was raising up a new leader. Saul had his opportunity as king. The Lord placed Saul in this position, but he was not committed to fulfilling his purpose. Be reminded that opportunities only last for a season. In this case, Saul was removed from the position of king because he misrepresented God's will as king. Saul missed God! He missed His plan. He missed His will. He missed his season. But most importantly, he missed His ways. Saul failed to appreciate the heart of God. God needed a king who would value His ways, and David was on his way to the throne.

Who's Responsible for Kings?

God is God over all. The Father is the source of everything. He is the Creator of everything that is, and nothing exists apart from Him. God takes care of His own. He provides for the birds, and He takes care of every flower that blooms. He is mindful of every human being. In short, creation represents His Kingdom. His will is that His created order would be maintained and expanded in the earth. In order to accomplish this, God created mankind and gave them dominion in the earth. Man was created to bring God glory, but more importantly, to represent His glory in the earth. The Father established His Kingdom in the earth and shared the responsibility of rulership with man. Every man must not only know God's will, but he must also have respect for His ways. If men truly knew their Father, they would appreciate His Word. One cannot know God as a Father yet disrespect His Word as a son.

God's heart has always been to have kings in the earth who reign with Him. These kings understand the Father's plan to see the Kingdom of Heaven manifest in the earth. The heart of the Father is to see His will done again on earth as it is in heaven. The challenge is that God must use men to accomplish this task. Man has been created a little lower than the angels, but to man has been given the responsibility to manage the affairs of the Father. Man is a steward over his Father's Kingdom, and God is mindful of him. If the Kingdom of Heaven is to come in the earth, it will take kings to make it a reality.

The nature of God is to cover. As king, God takes responsibility for everything He has created. In the same sense, God desires to cover His people. He must find a king who is strong and understands His intentions concerning His people. He must find a king who will not lose sight of His prophetic plan to make Israel His own. As His people, they are to be an example to all other nations of His faithfulness, power, and love. God seeks a king who will not forget His statutes. He must see a man who is limited by his nature yet is humble enough to acknowledge his dependency on Him. Men are God's designated kings. Along with the woman, man provides team leadership in the home,, but the man must take the lead in protecting his home. Men may not know God or even acknowledge Him, but every man is aware that he is under attack when it comes to leading in his own home. The man is the target when it comes to dividing kingdoms and ruining homes. Usually if the man can be bound and defeated, the rest of the family can be carried off.

Is this not the case with Goliath who represented the Philistines? If Goliath is defeated by Israel's representative, then all of the Philistine men and their families will become spoil, or the possession of the victor. The same is true in contrast. If the enemy wins the battle, then the strong men of Israel and their families become their possession. Isn't it ironic that there was no strong man in Israel who answered the challenge of Goliath? Even the king and his sons did not respond to the onslaught of the enemy. This is truly the example of a leadership gap. In fact, when leadership is needed most is when the enemy is at the doorstep of a man's house, threatening him, his family, and his God.

David realized this, and shortly thereafter everyone else took notice of it. Even King Saul was forced to acknowledge the spirit of David and the favor of God upon him.

Saul was afraid of David because the Lord was with David but had left Saul. So he sent David away from him and gave him command over a thousand men, and David led the troops in their campaigns.

In everything he did he had great success because the Lord was with him. When Saul saw how successful he was, he was afraid of him. But all Israel and Judah loved David, because he led them in their campaigns.

—1 Samuel 18:12–16

Leadership is often misunderstood and not appreciated. However, the test of a true leader is his ability to lead in hard times. The leader will always be appreciated when he leads victoriously in battle. Every wife appreciates the king in her home when the battle is over and the victory has been won. Every daughter gets a glimpse of the man she wants in her future as a result of the covering her father provides. There is not a son alive who does not yearn for a king in his life who trains him to be a king in the future. Everyone appreciates a king who leads, and they respect him even more when he is victorious. This does not mean that men are perfect. But men pursue perfection when they pursue the king inside of them. Israel and Judah loved David because of his leadership. When men are faithful as husbands, fathers, and as examples, those who are under their covering love them. When the family is provided for and protected from the enemies of life, the king is appreciated.

David had endured the learning process. He humbled himself and served a king whose motives were questionable at best. In addition, he was no longer permitted to return to his own home. He was cut off from his family and was eyed with suspicion by King Saul. He had to deal with the king's jealousy. He learned how to serve while perfecting his own survival. He found balance as a peacemaker caught between a father who despised him and a son who loved him as a brother. He had to learn not to become large in his own eyes while being hailed by the people. He had to endure the favor and love of all Israel and Judah while escaping the increasing wrath and hatred of King Saul.

When Saul realized that the Lord was with David and that his daughter Michal loved David, Saul became still more afraid of him, and he remained his enemy the rest of his days. The Philistine commander continued to go out to battle, and as often as they did, David met with more success than the rest of Saul's officers, and his name became well known.

—1 SAMUEL 18:28–30

Every man will be tested, and every king will be tried. David found himself experiencing all the accolades of notoriety while at the same time being scrutinized by the king. He must have been excited about what was before him but had to be watchful of what was behind him. In the midst of turmoil, God raises up kings. God needs kings because they will seek His heart, but God also needs kings because His people need leadership. There must be no leadership gaps because these gaps allow for the children to grow up not knowing the Lord or His promises towards them. Sons need fathers, women need covering, but men need kings. Without kings, kingdoms are divided, cities are ruined, and families are carried off as the spoil of their enemies.

Chapter 6

MEN STRENGTHENING MEN

The Original Intent

Men were always meant to strengthen men. Somewhere along life's journey, one generation to the next, men lost track of this great truth. Fathers were always to strengthen their sons. Brothers were supposed to strengthen their brothers. Grandfathers were to strengthen grandsons, and uncles were to strengthen their nephews. God has never changed His mind when it comes to men. Men must be strong because they represent the Father, but also because so many others depend on them. The Word of God reminds every man of the Father's intent for man: *As iron sharpens iron, so one man sharpens another* (Proverbs 27:17). Men are responsible to sharpen one another. This is the will of God for men. Notice that God is very particular about who sharpens men. According to the plan of God men are the ones identified to sharpen men. This is not meant to imply others cannot or do not sharpen men. In other words, it is understood that wives also sharpen husbands while sisters sharpen their brothers. Of course mothers sharpen their sons, but the point must not be lost: others can only sharpen the role or functions of a man.

When it comes to sharpening the "being" of a man, this requires another man. It is out of who the man is that he realizes what he is to do. This is why a woman cannot impart to a man his being. The man must receive this instruction from his father. This is expressly why the absence of the father in the home is having such widespread impact on sons. As a result, there are men today who are struggling to fulfill their expected roles but have never had their manhood affirmed by another man. Manhood is not the result of chronological age, nor is it the evidence of a man's ability to conceive a child. Manhood is never arrived at simply by external or visible variables. Rather, manhood is rooted in the revelation of purpose found only in the Creator's mind. A boy must know who a man is before he can become one. A young man must see for himself the true purpose for manhood before he can realize it in his own life. If a man is to avoid the snares of life, he must follow in the footsteps of another man who has overcome them. This is why the heavenly Father determined that only Jesus could be the example for all men; no other man understood it better. What other man has seen the Father? In short, what man is worthy or capable of fulfilling this awesome task besides the Lord?

God is a God of glory. Glory is what separates God from all of creation. His creation testifies of His glory. It was always meant to be this way. God desires to receive glory from everything He has made. Every created thing depends on Him. He created each and every thing with a divine purpose in mind. He has the right to expect the thing created to glorify Him in the earth. Man is the only thing He created with whom He shares His glory. This must be understood from two perspectives. The first perspective is that of dominion. God shared rulership responsibilities with mankind. In other words, man has the responsibility to maintain and increase the Father's influence in the earth; this is mankind's purpose. Together, the man and the woman are to rule, perpetuating God's plan while representing His will in the earth. The fulfillment of this great responsibility would bring glory to God; but there was an even greater responsibility given to mankind by the Father. Paul summarized it while writing to the church at Corinth. *A man ought not to cover his head, since he is the image and glory of God; but woman is the glory of the man* (1 Corinthians 11:7). Paul reveals that man is both the image and glory of God and simply reveals that the woman is the glory of the man. He does not repeat the statement made about the man in relationship to his Creator when referring to the woman.

It is understood that God created both the man and the woman in His image and His likeness. However, the context of this verse must be understood. Paul begins this chapter with these words: *Follow my example, as I follow the example of Christ* (1 Corinthians 11:1). This verse implies the priority of order. What seems to be emphasized here is not just the priority of following, but also the order in which one follows. Order is obviously very important to God. Paul continues with yet another revelation communicating the same principle. *Now I want you to realize that the head of every man is Christ, and the head of the woman is the man, and the head of Christ is God* (1 Corinthians 11:3). Again, Paul reveals the principle of order but illustrates his point by referring to headship. Headship was meant to clarify order. Simply put, if one is to operate in order, one must respect headship. Everything God created was created with headship in mind, and nothing created was meant to exist apart from headship. In this sense, Jesus became the supreme example of order as a result of His uncompromising respect for His own Headship, His Father. Jesus did absolutely nothing apart from His

Father. In the same way, a man must understand he was created to operate in God's ordained order. This can only be accomplished when men respect their headship. Paul reveals this is Jesus. He is the head of every man. When men operate apart from their headship, they are out of order. For men to live independently of their Creator is sin. But they must also have respect for the Father's order. Therefore, men must submit to the Lordship of Christ in order to glorify God. When this happens, men are viewed as the image and the glory of God.

In contrast, Paul continues by declaring: *But the woman is the glory of the man* (1 Corinthians 11:7b). This statement also represents Paul's attempt to emphasize order. He follows his statement with further clarification. *For man did not come from woman, but woman from the man; neither was man created for woman, but woman for man* (1 Corinthians 11:8–9). A point is being made in relationship to purpose. Every existing thing was created by God with a purpose in mind. Therefore, the man's purpose is understood in relationship to Christ since He is the head of every man. In similar fashion, the purpose of the woman is understood in relationship to the man since the head of the woman is man. Put another way, every woman lives under the headship of a man or a father figure. As a daughter, the woman is under the headship of an earthly father. As a wife, she is under the headship of a husband. Ultimately, all mankind is under the headship of God in Christ. Paul shares that mankind's ability to operate in order is the result of their submission to God.

The second perspective is critical to a man's understanding of manhood. The man was created by God to have a very specific place in the order of things. He was put on the earth to represent headship and to perpetuate order. Men must be taught about the order of God and their unique role in maintaining it. Women cannot impart this revelation to men because that would be out of order. The woman was created for man. Therefore, her purpose is associated to the man's purpose. As a result, she then is referred to as the glory of the man. The woman brings God glory when she helps fulfill the man's purpose. This requires teamwork, but more importantly, a deep appreciation for order and an uncompromising respect for headship. So many young men are confused today because they have never been taught these truths. Is anyone surprised that men are not leading?

Think about the mentality of the day. The popular perception is that the man is here for the woman. Have you ever heard the debate about who is responsible for the other? Without women there would be no men! Sounds too familiar, and it is this subconscious belief that has men confused about their own identity. Every man must realize his headship if he is to solve the leadership challenge. Every male must comprehend the order of God if he is to perpetuate his Father's influence in the family and in the home. Be reminded that when Eve led for the first time, order was forever challenged and headship was equally compromised.

Mankind was created to represent God's order and to be a witness of submission to and respect for headship. Sin subverted the original plan of God and demanded intervention from Him if order and headship were to be restored. Jesus became both the plan and the example to accomplish this. He submitted to the will of His Father and never disrespected His authority. Men must follow His example, understand these principles, and apply them in every area of life, realizing they are responsible to influence those they cover for the glory of God. Only men can fulfill this awesome responsibility because of the unique place they have been given by God. Again men must be reminded: *As iron sharpens iron, so one man sharpens another* (Proverbs 27:17).

The Original Motive

There are two questions that must be answered if men are to understand the original intent of the Father. Both questions are found in the Book of Beginnings and reveal glaring gaps in the hearts and minds of men today. These questions draw attention to the lack of leadership by men but also magnify the lack of understanding by men of their purpose and responsibility. The account of the relationship between the first brothers is recorded in Genesis 4. The result of this account is quite contrary to the original intent that was in the Father's heart for men. Both brothers find themselves confronted with authority and challenged by order. Cain and Abel must demonstrate their respect for who God is by the sacrifices they present to Him. More importantly, the sacrifices they present are a reflection of their understanding of God's headship of their lives. In other words, God is more focused on the heart of men as opposed to their response to Him.

The primary focus of a man must always be his heart towards God rather than his sacrifice to God. Whenever a man's heart is out of order, his sacrifice will be unacceptable as well. It is a fact that Cain did not find favor with God concerning his sacrifice, but the greater problem was his disposition. He was out of order! *But on Cain and his offering, He did not look with favor. So Cain was very angry, and his face was downcast* (Genesis 4:5). Men must be taught the life lesson that their response to any challenge is always more important than the challenge itself. Even God realizes this and provides every man the opportunity to overcome the challenge. *Then the LORD said to Cain, "Why are you angry? Why is your face downcast? If you do what is right, will you not be accepted? But if you do not do what is right, sin is crouching at your door; it desires to have you, but you must rule over it"* (Genesis 4:6–7).

Every man will be challenged. Life is full of challenges, and men have a greater share of challenges because they are responsible for others. Men don't do anything alone. Whatever a man does has the potential to affect others. This is true whether the man is preparing to lead or is already leading. This is why men must guard their hearts because they have the responsibility to lead. Men must value their role of headship because they will be held accountable for all who are entrusted to their care. Cain was not just angry, he was very angry. In addition, his face was downcast. A man's response will predict his direction. All too often the direction a man chooses is a reflection of his motives. Cain was visibly upset. He was upset because his sacrifice was not accepted by God, but was that really the source of his problem? The Father responded to Cain and addressed the root problem. His being upset was a symptom, but his anger had a root!

The word *symptom* is defined as "a change in bodily sensation, function, or appearance that dictates disorder, abnormality, or disease." God addressed Cain directly. *"Why are you angry? Why is your face downcast?"* (Genesis 4:6). God then responded with revelation: *"If you do what is right, will you not be accepted?"* (Genesis 4:7). This is clearly direction for all men. The only time men are not accepted by God is when they are not in right standing with God. Their dispositions are wrong; they are out of order. Something has begun to change in them. Access has been gained by some other influence, and things have become abnormal. That is called a disease. Before a disease can manifest complete control, there are usually signs communicating that a greater problem is on the way. God Himself explains this to Cain. If you don't do what is right, if you choose to go in the wrong direction, sin is crouching, ready to have its way with you. Like Cain, men have no other choice! Men must master the challenges of life. This can only be accomplished if men listen to the

Father. He has given them Christ as the example to follow. and He is the only legitimate head of every man.

The alternative is not hard to discern or predict. When a man chooses to ignore the instructions of the Lord, he becomes sick. The enemy, sin, finds access to his heart through the door of pride and rebellion. God did not give the man authority so he could claim control. Rather, God gave the man authority because he needed it to preserve order. Sin enters in and fulfills all its desire, making that man his slave. Many men are in this position because they have failed to heed the Word of God. Countless others are struggling because they have never been taught to revere and honor their fathers. They have no earthly examples to pattern their lives after. Because they have not learned to respect their earthly fathers, it is difficult for them to respect their heavenly Father. As a result, the leadership gap widens, and men's faces remain downcast. Whenever this happens, symptoms are overlooked and disease is permitted to cause sickness and even death. Men must be taught by other men that they represent headship. Men must impart to other men their unique place in God's divine order so that they respect authority. The enemy wants men to operate in darkness not realizing they represent authority in the earth. This is evident by the increase of violence of men against men. The enemy wants authority out of the way so he can have his way with those who lack covering. The evidence of this fact is that Cain killed his brother Abel. He was created to sharpen his brother, but instead he killed him. When men don't respect authority, they cannot appreciate manhood.

Men gravitate to authority because they were created to operate in dominion. All men assume they are supposed to be in charge, but few men realize that they are to cover. Men subconsciously wrestle with control. They are either overbearing or abusive or they retreat in frustration and confusion when their authority is challenged. There are generations of men today who want to be in control but have no understanding of the responsibility associated with it. Responsibility is a reflection of purpose. One is put in charge for a reason. There are always costs associated with leadership. Young men are growing up in this present age with no recollection of ancient landmarks. Their fathers are often not present to teach them about manhood. In reality, this lesson must be caught. This is why the presence of a man in the life of a boy is so necessary. That boy needs to see a godly example of manhood with his own eyes. He needs to have the opportunity to walk in the footsteps of another man and measure his foot in the print he is following. This causes a boy to dream about being like the man in his life. When a son decides to pattern his life after his father, he has caught hold of something more valuable than gold. This cannot be taught, but when a son learns to respect his father's wisdom, all the lessons he has been taught make sense. For the first time, he sees himself as a man and no longer a boy.

The eternal question the Father still asks is, *"Where is your brother?"* (Genesis 4:9). Men should know where their brothers are. Fathers should know where their sons are. This is not a question limited to geographic location. It is one that addresses the being of manhood. Where are sons today when there are no men in their lives? Where are fathers, and what direction are they providing to sons as they attempt to find their own identities? Where are the men? Mothers attend church with the children while the father remains in the background. Mothers are perceived as the disciplinarians in the home because the fathers are pre-occupied with work. Employment also limits the father's ability to support his son in the classroom or in recreational competitions. The heart-felt response is that most men can't tell you where their sons are. They have no real relationship with their sons. They don't spend time nurturing them. Fathers must exemplify manhood to their sons and then tell them what it is. The strategy has not changed. If a son is to know how to treat his wife, this lesson must be learned from how his father loves his mother. If the son is to comprehend what a provider looks like, what better example can he have than a father who takes care of his family?

Where are sons taught the truth about sacrifice? What school do they attend to learn about character or the value of their own reputation? Who teaches them about strength or responds to their need for adventure? Who responds to them when they mature and are faced with questions about their manhood? Who is responsible to show them what self-control looks like or what it means to consider others before themselves? Where does a young man learn that he is to protect his sister and respect women? Who tells him he is supposed to sharpen his brother? Can a boy learn how to manage money without an example? How does he learn to respond to his wife without a mentor? It is obvious that young men are learning the answers to these questions without fathers, but how much better would they be if they simply had a father's touch on their lives?

Where is your brother? The answer to this question is more important today than it was in Cain and Abel's time. In the beginning one man killed another man, but today life is not considered sacred, and death is far too common. Men have lost sight of this question altogether. Like Cain, they don't perceive this to be their responsibility. Cain's disposition was contrary to the will of his Creator. He lured his brother out into a field and then killed him. Where was Adam, their father, in this season of their lives? What difference could he have made if things were different? This is a relevant question even for today. Where are fathers, and what difference could they make in their sons' lives if they were only present?

The fact is that Cain killed his brother, and his parents' influence did not prevent it. Today, men cannot afford to repeat the mistakes of the past. Men must be strengthened if this curse is to be broken.

The first question was from God to Cain. The second question comes from Cain to the Father and carries equal weight. In response to the Lord's question: "Where is your brother Abel?" Cain replies: *"I don't know....Am I my brother's keeper?"* (Genesis 4:9–10). The first part of Cain's response is a lie. He knew where his brother was. In fact he had left him where he killed him. This situation is a startling example for all men today. Men have been left behind. It appears they are losing ground in many areas of life. Wives have been left behind. Men are visibly absent in the home. Increasing numbers of men have taken shortcuts and detours, blinding them to the benefits of an education and resulting in a lack of preparation for the future. In similar fashion, men continue to struggle in the workplace. Many young men have little sense of direction and have pursued quick fixes that compromise their potential and limit their ability to succeed. The greater problem is that men have left other men behind. Fathers have left sons behind while brothers have betrayed one another. This represents a mentality that has taken root in a generation of men. It must be addressed because the second part of the question is worse than the first. Cain cries: "Am I my brother's keeper?" Each man must know who his brother is and his role concerning his brother.

Am I my brother's keeper? It is apparent that Jesus understood the weight of this question. Of course He had a great respect for His headship. Peter portrayed the heart of the Father when he wrote: *The Lord is not slow in keeping his promise, as some understand slowness. Instead he is patient with you, not wanting anyone to perish, but everyone to come to repentance* (2 Peter 3:9). In order for this to be accomplished, someone must be responsible to teach and exemplify this truth to others. Jesus received this truth from His Father and then communicated and demonstrated it to His disciples. The Father placed great value on each human being and, through Christ, imparted this sense of value to all who would believe.

> *Then the King will say to those on his right, "Come, you who are blessed by my Father; take your inheritance, the kingdom prepared for you since the creation of the world. For I was hungry and you gave me something to eat, I was thirsty and you gave me something to drink. I was a stranger and you invited me in, I needed clothes and you clothed me, I was sick and you looked after me, I was in prison and you came to visit me." Then the righteous will answer him, "Lord, when did we see you hungry and feed you, or thirsty and give you something to drink? When did we see you a stranger and invite you in, or needing clothes and clothe you? When did we see you sick or in prison and go to visit you?" The King will reply, "Truly I tell you, whatever you did for one of the least of these brothers and sisters of mine, you did for me."*
>
> —Matthew 25:34–40

Jesus attempted to teach His followers that they were their brothers' keepers. Jesus exemplified the principle of order by representing His Father. In similar fashion, men are responsible to exemplify Christ to their families because He is their Head. Men must know that God's will for them involves their being responsible for others. This is imperative because the example cannot be replaced. If wives and children are to understand and appreciate this principle, it will be the result of the man providing covering for them. If sons are to value their manhood and understand their purpose, they must learn this principle from a father who has taught and nurtured them. But the best lessons are not the lessons taught, but rather the lessons caught. This is why the absence of fathers is having such a negative impact upon families today.

There comes a time in a man's life where he must be encouraged by another man. Men can also be encouraged by women, but there are some realities in a man's life that a woman cannot respond to. This is also true for women. In fact, women seem to understand this principle naturally. They are more prone to come together and find encouragement among themselves. In contrast, men tend to attempt success on their own. Men seem to believe they can handle life's challenges alone but must be careful lest they become deceived thinking they can overcome their challenges in their natural strength. At this point men become frustrated and must realize they need support and encouragement. This is also the place where women experience frustration. They attempt to support men but are confused by their negative responses. This is a reality because the woman is attempting to strengthen the man when this is not her sphere of influence. She can encourage him, but all too often he does not respond because he is in a battle for his own manhood. The reason the woman cannot strengthen him is because this kind of battle requires another man. Only another man can affirm him because he understands the weight of having to be strong for everyone else. It is more of a spiritual challenge than it is a physical reality.

The Original Principle

The word *principle* means "a rule or code of conduct." It also involves a "devotion to such a code." This is important because principles apply to many areas of life. There is a purpose for the principle and a context in which the principle is expected to work. There are principles in life that enhance a man's understanding. Put another way, there are things in life that books cannot teach a person. Usually one goes to school to be trained and is often taught theory. However, there are some realities in life that theory does not address. In these situations, one needs insight that only comes from another person who has traveled the road he is now on. This is why the principle is real. Men must strengthen men because there are blind spots in the road of life that were never addressed by books. There may be holes in the road being traveled, and insight is required if one is to avoid the distractions. Finally, a young man needs an older man's touch to show him how to avoid the pitfalls of life. Men guiding other men simply confirms that men are their brothers' keepers.

First Chronicles 11:10 illustrates this principle. It reads: *These were the chiefs of David's mighty warriors—they, together with all Israel, gave his kingship strong support to extend it over the whole land, as the* LORD *had promised.* The King James Version reads this way: *These also are the chief of the mighty men whom David had, who strengthened themselves with him in his kingdom, and with all Israel, to make him king, according to the word of the* LORD *concerning Israel.* This KJV text reveals a principle: Men only get stronger when they run with other men. A man will become like the company he keeps. This is why it is so important for a man to be discerning about who he runs with. Fathers are needed in the home to sharpen their sons, teaching them the value of strength in the context of relationships. In contrast, the absence of male role models in the home may produce men who fail to associate strength with manhood. Boys must have an innate example of strength. This is not meant to imply that women are not strong, but men must understand that their strength is part of their purpose. A man's strength exists so he can fulfill his purpose in covering his family. His strength prevents the enemy from robbing his house and stealing his goods. Fathers must impart purpose to their sons lest they abuse their gift of strength. If there were ever a time when men were needed, it is now.

God's will for Saul, the first man chosen to be king, was that he would simply become a king. Saul would have to understand the order of God to accomplish this. Saul was anointed king to represent God before the people. In other words, the Father's will was to be more important than the will of the king. Saul needed to realize he was a part of the Father's kingdom. This fact alone would prevent confusion. Saul's rebellion against God was wrong. Becoming big in his own eyes was a mistake, but the bigger problem was a divided kingdom. Saul allowed access to the enemy by his unwillingness to submit to his King. When the people asked for a king, they, in essence, rejected God as their king. When men reject the Lord as king over their lives, they unwillingly establish their own kingdom. But every kingdom divided against itself will suffer ruin. Saul missed it. He forgot he was subject to the King of kings. God cannot allow men to live in rebellion and remain in His Kingdom. This is the reason why the kingdom was taken from Saul and given to another man. Men who are outside the will of God have no relationship with Him. As a result, they are also outside His Kingdom. In this position, a man is not able to fulfill his divine purpose. His purpose is only realized within the context of the Kingdom of God submitted to its King.

Every kingdom must have a king. God gave Saul the responsibility of leading and protecting Israel from its enemies. Study of the text reveals that the Philistine nation was at war against Israel. In his final battle at Mount Gilboa, Saul was mortally wounded. This represented a severe blow to Israel because then it had no king. Equally devastating was the death of his sons. Not only had Israel lost its king, but it had also had lost an entire family. Saul's sons died with him, and that meant the end of his legacy. There was no one from his house to succeed him.

> *All Israel came together to David at Hebron and said, "We are your own flesh and blood. In the past, even while Saul was king, you were the one who led Israel on their military campaigns. And the LORD your God said to you, 'You will shepherd my people Israel, and you will become their ruler.'" When all the elders of Israel had come to King David at Hebron, he made a covenant with them at Hebron before the LORD, and they anointed David king over Israel, as the LORD had promised through Samuel.*
> —1 CHRONICLES 11:1–3; 2 SAMUEL 5:1–2

Notice that the leadership of Israel was aware that David was supposed to be king. They even imply they were aware of this fact while Saul was still alive. These leaders refer to David as the shepherd of God's people. They also recognize that David had been chosen by God. This time the leaders accepted God's choice. God had already made up His mind concerning who would be the next king in Israel. The Bible reveals: *Saul died because he was unfaithful to the LORD; he did not keep the Word of the LORD and even consulted a medium for guidance, and did not inquire of the LORD. So the LORD put him to death and turned the kingdom over to David son of Jesse* (1 Chronicles 10:13–14). These verses are important for every man. If one is not careful, he will conclude that God's position concerning Saul was in response to his unfaithfulness. Like Saul, all men have made mistakes, even David. However, the emphasis here must not be overlooked. Saul not only made a mistake, but he somehow came to a place where he no longer consulted God for guidance. Another way to say this is Saul failed to repent. Be reminded, when he was confronted by

Samuel, he responded by declaring he had done everything he had been commanded to do. His lack of humility ultimately caused him to lose the kingship. Somewhere along the way, Saul went from a position of pride to one of total independence. How could God allow a man to represent him who no longer sought Him for direction?

What happens when those under a king lose their king? They go looking for another king. In spite of the fact Saul had died, the Philistines were still at war with Israel. The leadership of Israel was desperate to find a king. This was a time of confusion and disorder. The king's primary responsibility was to lead the people, but this also involved restoring order. David acknowledged their request and made a compact with them. As a result, these leaders anointed David king over Israel. This action was simply the confirmation of what the Lord had promised through Samuel. David's responsibility was to address the security of his nation. He would have to organize his leadership and implement strategic plans preventing the enemy from spoiling the land. This would require men who would strengthen David as the new king in Israel.

Regardless of the call or role of a man, he will need to be strengthened. Even kings need to be strengthened. God does not wait on men because they rarely admit their needs. The Bible confirms that warriors came to David, but in reality, they were sent by God. For example, Scripture declares: *Where there is no revelation, the people cast off restraint; but blessed is the one who heeds wisdom's instruction* (Proverbs 29:18). God revealed His plan to David. This is called revelation. This revelation was not for David alone, but for Israel as well. Notice God had already referred to him as a shepherd over His people. David was a king well before it was confirmed by Israel. This revelation, however, took David from covering a flock to covering a nation. Every man has been anointed a king by the

Father. God has shared authority with man by giving him dominion over all His creation. Each man must realize there are moments in life where others will come to him and confirm his kingship. This is the time for a man to step up.

God needed a king who would submit to His plan. If David understood the heart of God, he could be trusted with God's plan. If God could trust David to obey His will and lead His people, He would send them to David so they could strengthen him. God promised David his seed would be represented on the throne of His Kingdom if he would obey Him and not forget Him. Notice that the promise involved God's Kingdom but made allowance for David's family to share the throne. God wills that men would be a part of His legacy in the earth. David realized God was obviously talking about a kingdom beyond his lifetime. As a result, David saw God's people differently. He also saw the kingship differently. It is here that David began to appreciate the anointing of God. David realized it was the anointing on his life that qualified him. The most precious thing in his life became his relationship with the Father. Every man must experience this revelation as well. Men must always depend on God for guidance. Every leader needs guidance to help him fulfill the call of God upon his life.

Beyond the men who came to David to help him in battle, there were chiefs even among them. What was their purpose? Why is this important? Their role is described very specifically. *These were the chiefs of David's mighty warriors—they, together with all Israel, gave his kingship strong support to extend it over the whole land, as the LORD had promised* (1 Chronicles 11:10). These chiefs literally helped David build the kingdom. By working together with David and all Israel, they established Israel as a model of the Kingdom of God in the earth. David, as king, symbolized the starting point for the coming eternal kingdom. Israel served as the forerunner to God's Kingdom in the earth. Through Israel would come another king, and David would be referred to as a father to this new king. David had seen eternity, and it had changed him. In spite of his human frailty, he never lost sight of God's promise. He always depended on the Lord even when he strayed. The chiefs were called to the kingdom while men were called to the king. The men were called to strengthen David in battle while the chiefs were called to support him in establishing the kingdom.

Most men realize their struggles but fail to acknowledge their calling. If men are to realize their calling, they must be strengthened by chiefs. Every man must be able to distinguish between men who come to help in battle and those who are called to help with the vision. Those called chiefs are valuable because they not only strengthen the king but also rally the people in support of the vision. The king is responsible for the army and the people. There are men who are conscious of the battle only, but the king needs leaders who assist with the people. The victory is won in battle, but the hearts of the people are won in service. It is important to win in battle because the man is called to establish a kingdom. When a man becomes a husband, he establishes a kingdom. Though he will experience struggle, his responsibility is to always trust the Father for direction. He must never become self-dependent or seek other sources for guidance. Like David, every man must value his relationship with the Lord and guard and cherish his anointing. May each man discern between men and chiefs to help him secure his kingdom.

Chapter 7

WHEN MEN RUN

Why Men Run

f the truth were told, it would reveal that men run. In fact, men have been guilty of running away from their responsibilities for some time. Men have been known to even run away from God. *But Jonah ran away from the LORD and headed for Tarshish. He went down to Joppa, where he found a ship bound for that port. After paying the fare, he went aboard and sailed to Tarshish to flee from the LORD* (Jonah 1:3). Jonah serves as an example of the rebellious spirit in man. God commanded Jonah to go to the city of Nineveh and preach against it, but Jonah refused to obey the Lord's command. His alternative was to run. The sad reality was he could not outrun the Lord. Jonah ran from God and His will for his life. However, there are other reasons why men run.

Moses was also a man who was on the run. Why did Moses need to run? *Then Moses was afraid and thought, "What I did must have become known." When Pharaoh heard of this, he tried to kill Moses, but Moses fled from Pharaoh and went to live in Midian, where he sat down by a well* (Exodus 2:14b–15). Moses was called by God to bring His people Israel out of Egypt. The children of Israel cried unto the Lord because of their oppression in Egypt. Moses was raised in Pharaoh's house but could not shake his own identity as a Hebrew. As a result, he was compelled to defend his own people from the oppressor. He killed an Egyptian who was beating a Hebrew, and that made him a fugitive in Egypt. He fled from Pharaoh who wanted him dead. There are many men who are running from their mistakes or the consequences of them. Many others have left their homes with no potential of returning. These men continue to run because their enemies are consistently searching for them.

The reasons why men run can be complicated. David serves as an example here. One of the major reasons why men run is change. When men don't know the Lord, it is difficult for them to handle change. If a man is insecure about his own identity and his purpose, change can cause him to become confused about his leadership and his responsibilities. At no other time is the impact of a man's confusion felt more than when he fails to realize his measure of rule or his sphere of influence. No man can lead effectively when he questions his own authority or doubts his influence. This challenge is being witnessed more and more in the family as men choose to run because they don't feel appreciated, needed, or respected. Men must be reminded again of their leadership role in the home. They must realize there is accountability in the home. However, if men are going to be held accountable in the home, they must also be taught they have the right to influence. In other words, those who hold them accountable should also respect their influence. When men are scrutinized and disrespected by those for whom they are responsible, the end result usually will be an exodus. This is important because you cannot talk to a man without talking to a family. If he does not have a literal family, one is still in him. In similar fashion, you cannot talk to a man without talking to his relationships. Each man is destined to be responsible for someone else or to become responsible at some time in the future. In any case, men must realize there is life in them because they are seed bearers. The enemy always pursues the seed bearer. The weight of responsibility will always fall to the head, and men were created to hold this position. Most men are not aware of this reality because they have never been taught about leadership or never had a role model to follow.

In an ideal world, all men would have a healthy respect for authority. Every man would fully comprehend his role of headship, and no man would be confused about his role as provider and protector. In similar fashion, each man would embrace his responsibility as the visionary while striving to be the strong man who prevents the enemy from destroying his household. Every man would be educated, aware of the fact he is the source and originator of his family. His initiative to live up to eternal expectations would no longer be the result of external variables but driven from an internal awareness of his own value. He would fully comprehend his worth in the context of family and run with assurance knowing he is well able to fulfill his ordained role as the man. Finally, this man would be submitted to the Lordship of Christ. His responsibility would be to represent his King to those under his authority and influence. These men would never run from their commitments or their created role as fathers.

When Running Seems to Be the Only Alternative

Unfortunately there are times in the lives of men when they seem to have no other alternative but to run. They cannot succeed regardless of how hard they try. They are caught in circumstances beyond their control. It is usually in these kinds of situations that the sovereignty of God is witnessed.

That day David fled from Saul and went to Achish king of Gath. But the servants of Achish said to him, "Isn't this David, the king of the land? Isn't he the one they sing about in their dances: 'Saul has slain his thousands, and David his tens of thousands'?" David took these words to heart and was very much afraid of Achish king of Gath.
—1 SAMUEL 21:10–12

David had no good choice. He was being pursued by Saul, the king of Israel. This obviously hurt because Saul represented family. What do men do when they are no longer accepted at home? What realities confront men when their own families shut doors in their faces? This family was divided. Jonathan, the son of King Saul, was supportive of David. Many in strategic positions also supported David. In fact, there were many in the general populace who recognized David's potential and applauded his accomplishments. This sad reality became obvious as a result of the outward praises of the people toward David. This caused confusion where King Saul was concerned. He was convinced David was the enemy. King Saul used his position to influence those under his authority against David. Immediately, David became an outlaw among his own people, a bounty was set on his head, and those under the influence of the king were convinced that David was the enemy.

David found himself in a no-win situation. What had he done to deserve this? All he had done was serve the king. He had submitted to every command and followed every order. He never asked to be sent to serve the king. He never pursued the king's favor nor did he have a hidden agenda to become the king's armor-bearer. He simply was doing what he thought was right. How many men have tried to simply do what is right only to find themselves in more chaos? What does a man do when he feels totally committed to his own, but then is rejected, misrepresented, and falsely accused? This is the circumstance now confronting David. All of these unfortunate circumstances and events brought David to a moment in time when he must do something regardless of how desperate it might appear. The record refers to this moment as "that day." In other words, the day came when David recognized his tomorrow was in jeopardy. He had to do something now!

David chose to run. That day had finally come. He could no longer trust his life to Saul. David did not know who his enemies were, and that was a sad reality because his own family had become his enemy. This represented ultimate frustration. What had happened to cause this kind of confusion? What had he done to find himself in this position? These are the questions men raise within themselves when they attempt to do everything they know to do and it still is not enough. These are the feelings men experience when they sacrifice all they have for others and still are not appreciated. It seems their labor is in vain. This was the plight David faced. He had laid down his all, put his life on the line, yet now he was the enemy. He was being pursued by men he had led in battle. He was falsely accused by people who ought to have known him better than anyone else. Furthermore, he had no options to defend himself. This surely had to hurt because his track record was sure and his reputation was beyond reproach. Yet in spite of this, he still was forced to run.

Think about this. How many men do you know who have run away from their role as a father? What man in your experience has failed to live up to expectations placed on him? What circumstances have brought a generation of men to a day when they question their own value? How have we arrived at that day when young men have no idea of foundational truths about their purpose, their identity, or their worth? Rather than pursue the answer, rather than accept the challenge, far too many men have chosen to run.

When the day arrives and men feel they can no longer remain where they are, then where do they run to? Desperate times call for desperate measures. David ran from Saul to Achish. That was a serious problem. David ran from his own people to the enemy. Achish was Philistine! Even his own servants questioned his acceptance of David. Notice they were not confused about David's identity or reputation. They told King Achish who David was. He was the king that the people sang about. Surely he could not do anything positive in the eyes of the Philistines. They had negative intent in their hearts toward David and nothing was going to change that. This problem still exists today. In fact, it is being magnified. Young men are leaving the security of their families, fleeing from those who love them, literally running away from home to the enemy. Unfortunately many of these young men find no favor among the enemy. Men must be reminded that the enemy is the enemy for good reason. The enemy intends no good for them. Only the favor of God can keep men in the midst of the enemy. The enemy has already made up his mind concerning these sons. His intent has not changed. His desire is to destroy the seed, and now the seed is in his territory. The best solution to this dilemma is to make men feel comfortable at home. Many sons can be saved if they simply never flee to the enemy's camp. Regardless of the situation young men face, they must realize the enemy is not a viable alternative.

God was with David. David had no other alternative but to flee. He had nowhere else to go but to the enemy. There were not many at home he could trust. This was truly a no-win situation. However, there is a positive side even in the worst of situations. David had been chosen by God to be the next king in Israel, a fact that had become widely known, and there was a great expectation among the people. Even the enemy was aware of this fact. It was up to God to keep David so His purpose would prevail. In other words, men should realize that sometimes they must endure seasons in foreign territory under enemy influence. But regardless of this reality, they must not forget the Lord or become captivated by their enemy. Maybe this is what David was testifying about when he wrote: *You prepare a table before me in the presence of my enemies. You anoint my head with oil; my cup overflows* (Psalm 23:5). David was anointed and found favor in the sight of his enemy because he realized who he was in God and remained humble in his own eyes. He believed God and was convinced every promise God had made to him would come to pass in his lifetime. Men must remain faithful to the promises of God even when it seems they have been forsaken. They must make up their minds to stand on the Word of God even if it means running to the enemy's camp for a season. Men must not give up on the promises of God to sustain them even in the midst of trials. Fathers must communicate to their sons that God will prove Himself on their behalf. He will not allow their enemies to triumph over them. God has not changed His mind where men are concerned. Running was never God's will for men.

The Cost of Running

Running may be necessary at times, but it is never good. Running is always associated with a cost. When men run, someone is going to pay for it. This may involve a family, a wife, or a child, but someone will suffer as a result of men running. Most of the time it is the man himself who suffers the greatest loss. He will pay the greatest price for his decision to flee. Remember that when Saul and his sons died in battle, all the men of

Israel ran. They left their cities and their wives and children to the whims of the Philistines. The Philistines came and occupied the abandoned cities. Their abandoned families suffered under the oppression of the Philistines. There are many families suffering right now because they too have been abandoned. There is no man in the home to stand against the enemy whose desire is to exploit the family and destroy the home. It was never the Father's will that men would run, leaving their loved ones behind.

David was convinced he had no other alternative than to run. He had consulted with Jonathan, and it was confirmed that Saul meant him harm. Jonathan had given David a signal alerting him to the disposition of his father, Saul.

> *In the morning Jonathan went out to the field for his meeting with David. He had a small boy with him, and he said to the boy, "Run and find the arrows I shoot." As the boy ran, he shot an arrow beyond him. When the boy came to the place where Jonathan's arrow had fallen, Jonathan called out after him, "Isn't the arrow beyond you?" Then he shouted, "Hurry! Go quickly! Don't stop!" The boy picked up the arrow and returned to his master. (The boy knew nothing of all this; only Jonathan and David knew.) Then Jonathan gave his weapons to the boy and said, "Go, carry them back to town." After the boy had gone, David got up from the south side of the stone and bowed down before Jonathan three times, with his face to the ground. Then they kissed each other and wept together—but David wept the most. Jonathan said to David, "Go in peace, for we have sworn friendship with each other in the name of the LORD, saying, 'The LORD is witness between you and me, and between your descendants and my descendants forever.'" Then David left, and Jonathan went back to town.*
>
> —1 SAMUEL 20:35–42

Jonathan was not convinced his father meant to kill David. Jonathan would inquire of his father, Saul, and find out for himself what his true motive was concerning David. Once he found out, he would communicate his findings to David. They agreed to meet at a certain place, and Jonathan would let David know what he had found out. Jonathan used the position of his arrows to communicate with David whether he was safe to remain or not. Per the accounts, he cried out: "The arrow is beyond you!" This was veiled language, but he was updating David to the reality he had discovered. "Go quickly! Don't stop! Hurry!" That was all the confirmation David needed. He was now assured of King Saul's intentions toward him. Jonathan, the son of the king and his closest friend had brought him this alarming news. This was painful to both Jonathan and David. They were acutely aware of the future and the fact things were going to be different. One thing was sure; David would ultimately become king. So they reaffirmed their covenant to each other in relation to their descendants. David wept the most because he was not sure of what the future held for his friend Jonathan. David knew Jonathan meant him no harm. He had supported him against all odds. Both their lives were now in the Lord's hands. Unfortunately for Jonathan, his future was tied to his father, and one thing was sure. His father would not remain the king of Israel.

On the other hand, David had to face the grim news that Saul meant to kill him. There was no safe place in Israel where he could hide. His greatest friend, the son of the king, had now confirmed what he already knew. His choices were limited. He must run regardless of the consequences. The outcome of his decision to run could be worse than the decision to remain. His present situation was truly beyond his control. All he could do at that point was to trust the Lord. The prophet had shown up at his home unannounced, and he had been anointed to become king in the presence of his father and his brothers. Somehow he found himself a servant in the house of the king himself. Then he became an armor-bearer and was drawn even closer to the king. He realized God was with him and blessed him. He found favor in the sight of all Israel. But what went wrong? How had things changed so quickly? He was not the enemy and had done nothing to deserve that reputation. He then found himself on the outside and there was no one who could right the wrongs he was experiencing.

What do men do when they are innocent yet condemned? Who do men turn to when their reputations have been tarnished and there is nothing they can do about it? David provided some insight for all men when he wrote: *The LORD watches over you—the LORD is your shade at your right hand; the sun will not harm you by day, nor the moon by night. The LORD will keep you from all harm—he will watch over your life; the LORD will watch over your coming and going both now and forevermore* (Psalm 121:5–8). David turned his attention to the Lord. He must trust his life to his Creator and believe Him to somehow bring order out of the confusion of his life. So he runs, not knowing the outcome but trusting in the Word of the Lord.

There are some lessons to be learned from running. Every man can benefit from these lessons as he puts his trust in the Lord. Men must always prepare for change and realize that some changes will not be good. This is why men must have God on their side. Men must have a relationship with their Creator because, when change comes, the promises of God remain sure. Change does not alter a man's created purpose. Only God can keep men when their world is suddenly turned upside down. When all else fails, a man's faith in God will sustain him.

The first lesson men learn from running is found in 1 Samuel 21:1 which reads: *David went to Nob, to Ahimelek the priest. Ahimelek trembled when he met him, and asked, "Why are you alone? Why is no one with you?"* Men must realize when they run, they usually run alone. This is the first lesson and is most important. When men are faced with critical choices in times of crisis, they usually make decisions resulting in their solitude. In these moments of isolation, a man discovers who he is and what he is made of. Each man will experience moments of loneliness and seasons of isolation. He cannot take his wife and family with him through these desert experiences. He cannot confide in his wife nor does he share with other men. He has been taught he must endure these trials alone, and hopefully he will come out the better for it. Jesus Himself was driven into the wilderness for a similar season of testing. There is no escaping these moments. A man must learn who he truly depends on and what he really believes. This can only be accomplished in the fire of solitude. Every man can remember these moments in his life. He must be totally dependent on the grace of God if he is to survive at all.

The second lesson men learn when they run comes from a question David asked Ahimelech. *Now then, what do you have on hand? Give me five loaves of bread, or whatever you can find* (1 Samuel 21:3). It is obvious David was hungry. He did not have the opportunity to prepare food for his journey, and he may have become weak because he had no food while on the run. Crisis situations do not allow for proper preparation. Most often one is simply consumed with survival. As a result, one will experience hunger while running. All too often men attempt to fulfill their responsibilities while malnourished. Men only need to acknowledge they have needs and pursue God's promise to supply those needs. Men will always be better off when they accept the fact that God uses others to meet their needs. In fact, men will experience fulfillment when they realize it is God's intention to use them to meet the needs of others, especially other men. If this is to become each man's experience, he must also find nourishment for his needs. No one can continuously give without receiving. God's heart is to nourish men. The enemy wants men to think they can be men alone. This is deception. Men may be alone for a season, but God's will is that they would sharpen each other. Men must find support from each other. When men find themselves alone and in need, this is usually an indication they need to seek out other men who will sharpen them.

It is necessary for men to have relationships with other men. In this way, men develop friendships that will last and endure conflict and confusion. In times of crisis these relationships will be the difference between success and failure. Today many men fail to succeed because they don't have these kinds of relationships. Again, this point only highlights the importance of the father in the home. This is imperative for sons because they need an example of leadership in crisis seasons. If sons are to know how to deal with crises, they must learn this from a father figure in their lives. There are those who believe that sons can learn these lessons from mothers in the absence of fathers. The problem with this scenario is this situation itself is crisis. Far too many sons become confused about their role in this familiar type of crisis. Young men either attempt to take on the role of a father or subconsciously they are pulled on for the same purpose. This situation does not represent a nurturing opportunity for a son. When a father is in the home, a son has the opportunity to witness the example of his father providing without any pressure for him to be anything other than a son. In fact, the father may provide hands-on opportunities for his son by permitting him to share in the resolution of a crisis situation. In any case, men need other men in their lives who represent a positive example and who are committed to their well-being especially when they are in turmoil.

A third lesson men learn when they run is also an important one. David was on the run. He had no one with him at this time. He had come to Nob to Ahimelech, the priest. He was famished and in great need of food. Ahimelech responded to his request for food. However, they were not alone. *Now one of Saul's servants was there that day, detained before the LORD; he was Doeg the Edomite, Saul's head shepherd* (1 Samuel 21:7). Isn't it amazing when men run they are never free from their enemies? David had fled from Saul but was seen by one of Saul's servants. Life is so complicated, and men tend to think running away might really solve their problems. The reality is there are always reminders of why they are running regardless of where they find themselves. This is why men need genuine relationships with other men who are committed to them. When men run, they are not sure who is for them or against them.

David recognized Doeg and realized he was not safe. How are men to respond when they are alone but have been identified? They have been spotted by those who are on their enemy's side. David did what most men might do when faced with this kind of dilemma. *David asked Ahimelek, "Don't you have a spear or sword here? I haven't brought my sword or any other weapon, because the king's mission was urgent"* (1 Samuel 21:8). David was not only alone and hungry, but he also had no means of protecting himself. In the midst of crisis, he had run without any regard for his own needs. He found himself without a weapon. He was in the midst of his enemy. He realized his life was in jeopardy and he had to find a way to defend himself. Today, multitudes of men are on the run and have no weapons to protect themselves. Many more men are on the run without a weapon and only realize it when they are confronted by their enemies. The greatest deception here is they think they can overcome their enemies in their own strength. The sad reality, however, reveals the battles they are fighting require different weapons altogether. If men are to succeed in today's world, they must have spiritual weapons because the battles they are involved in are not carnal. Their battles will not be won in their natural strength. Their abilities, gifts, and even their experiences are not sufficient against this enemy.

The priest replied, "The sword of Goliath the Philistine, whom you killed in the Valley of Elah, is here; it is wrapped in a cloth behind the ephod. If you want it, take it; there is no sword here but that one." David said, "There is none like it; give it to me" (1 Samuel 21:9). David was running from King Saul. He had been spotted by the king's servant, and the only weapon available to him was the sword of Goliath, the Philistine he had killed. When men run, there is always a price to be paid. It is at this point that David decided to go to Achish, king of Gath. The text specifically states: *That day he fled from Saul and went to Achish, king of Gath.* Much was at stake, and David realized how urgent this moment really was. He had no choice but to run. He could not remain where he was now that he had been seen. It would not be long before Saul would be informed and make his move to capture David. There would be no such thing as a fair trial if he had been apprehended by Saul. He ran to Achish even though this was not beneficial. Achish's men identified him as the king of the land and rehearsed the words of the songs sung by the women as David returned from battle. David realized his enemy was just as serious as King Saul. As a result, he had to fake insanity in order to escape potential conflict. The sad reality is David was a man on the run with nowhere to go.

David was, however, not the only one on the run. It cannot be over-emphasized how one man's decision to run can affect others. *David left Gath and escaped to the cave of Adullam. When his brothers and his father's household heard about it, they went down to him there* (1 Samuel 22:1). It appeared that David's loss of favor also affected his family. Remember that David's family had experienced exceptional favor as a result of David's defeating the giant Goliath, but things had also turned sour for them. They found it necessary to leave their home and join David. Their decision must be pondered if one is to fully understand the context. David's new home is a cave. His brothers and apparently all his father's household chose to leave their homes and join him in a cave. Something is seriously wrong in the land of Israel. Whenever there are problems, there is also a demand for a leader. King Saul was obviously struggling to lead. His failure to provide leadership may have come as a result of his distraction involving David. In essence, King Saul had declared David his enemy, and now all of his attention was consumed with David. The people, especially the men, were disillusioned with this crisis. *All those who were in distress or in debt or discontented gathered around him [David], and he became their commander. About four hundred men were with him* (1 Samuel 22:2). Men began to leave Saul and now pursue David whom they had identified as a leader even though he was on the run. These men were described as those in distress, in debt, or just discontented. They apparently concluded that Saul was not the man needed to sharpen them. Saul was viewed as the king, but not as a leader. However, not every man is willing to change his allegiance in the midst of crisis. This is an apparent reality today as many young men choose to remain with negative or poor examples of leadership. They too are in distress, in debt or discontented. They are desperately looking for alternative sources of genuine leadership. If they cannot find authentic leadership, they will leave the comfort of their homes to live in caves.

What had David done to change his perception by the men of Israel? His reputation as a warrior had not changed. No one could undo the victories he had won. It was his leadership that had made those victories a reality. Many men still remembered how they must have felt to witness a child, by all known standards, defeat a seasoned warrior who just happened to be a giant as well. They reluctantly recalled their unwillingness to step forward in response to the challenges of Goliath. Yet this young shepherd boy had not only declared his intentions but had miraculously backed them up. David was a leader, and no lie could change that fact. He knew who he was, and no jealous king could steal that knowledge from him. Most every man remembered when he decided to pursue the enemy. They had gone from "then men," only engaging the enemy after their giant had been slain, to men who would now place themselves in peril by declaring their allegiance to a king on the run.

This was no small decision for any man. Any decision made in support of a man on the run could prove fatal for that man and his entire family.

> *Now Saul heard that David and his men had been discovered. And Saul was seated, spear in hand, under the tamarisk tree on the hill at Gibeah, with all his officials standing at his side. He said to them, "Listen, men of Benjamin! Will the son of Jesse give all of you fields and vineyards? Will he make all of you commanders of thousands and commanders of hundreds? Is that why you have all conspired against me? No one tells me when my son makes a covenant with the son of Jesse. None of you is concerned about me or tells me that my son has incited my servant to lie in wait for me, as he does today."*
> —1 Samuel 22:6–8

These are not the words of a true leader. King Saul had become completely consumed by his own insecurities toward David. He had literally slandered his own son, falsely accused his own leadership, and exposed his true motive for pursuing David. Each leader most likely was asking himself what the benefit of receiving all these privileges from the king was. David had been given all of these things as well, and he was no better for it. All of these men, including Jonathan, were paying a price for the lack of leadership by the king of Israel. The sad fact is they chose to remain with the king.

But Doeg the Edomite, who was standing with Saul's officials, said, "I saw the son of Jesse come to Ahimelek son of Ahitub at Nob. Ahimelek inquired of the LORD for him; he also gave him provisions and the sword of Goliath the Philistine" (1 Samuel 22:9–10). In short, King Saul was consumed with the belief that others were conspiring with David, who was lying in wait and rebelling against him.

King Saul called Ahimelech before him and accused him of being just as much an enemy as David was. As a result, King Saul threatened Ahimelech and his father's family. *But the king said, "You will surely die, Ahimelek, you and your whole family." Then the king ordered the guards at his side: "Turn and kill the priests of the LORD, because they too have sided with David. They knew he was fleeing, yet they did not tell me." But the king's officials were not willing to raise a hand to strike the priests of the LORD* (1 Samuel 22:16–17). Something was seriously wrong when the king's own officials decided not to follow his commands. It had become obvious to everyone the problem was really King Saul. His obsession with David had gotten out of hand. Anyone who had anything to do with David was in trouble, and yet most of King Saul's men didn't agree with him that David was guilty. Still they were content to remain under the influence of a king whose position no longer represented true leadership.

The king then ordered Doeg, "You turn and strike down the priests." So Doeg the Edomite turned and struck them down. That day he killed eighty-five men who wore the linen ephod. He also put to the sword Nob, the town of the priests, with it men and women, its children and infants, and its cattle, donkeys and sheep (1 Samuel 22:18–19). What example of leadership had these men witnessed? Remember, someone will always pay a price when men run. Saul had no problem following through with his own command. He was responsible for the deaths of everyone and apparently everything in the city of Nob. He not only directed the slaughter of all the priests, he also gave the command to butcher the inhabitants of Nob. This is so ironic. Is this not the same man God commanded to destroy the Amalekites? But history records his failure to obey the command of the Lord. Saul misrepresented the Lord before the people, elevating himself as the source of authority. Now this mistake is further magnified by his willful determination to kill David and anyone else he assumes is affiliated with him. This serves as another example of what can happen when a man becomes bigger in his own eyes than the will of God for his life. Saul was not willing to obey the commands of the Lord and totally destroy the Amalekites, but he had no problem shedding the innocent blood of the inhabitants of Nob all because he was obsessed with killing David. He had taken his obsession to another level by killing anyone he assumed to be in alliance with David. There must be an end to this madness. Unfortunately, it would require a heavy price of retribution and include the death of Saul's sons. Saul himself was on the run from the will of God. Someone always pays when men run.

Are Men Supposed to Run?

Every boy and every young man has heard the words *"don't you run."* This implies he is to stay and fight. The more subtle implication is if he runs, he is not a man. This conclusion is widely accepted. Men don't run! Rather, they prove their manhood by staying and fighting. This deception has been taken to the extreme in our society today. Our communities continue to witness countless homicides involving young men who are under the influence of this kind of thinking. Young men have died needlessly because they fought for a cause that had no real meaning and stood for reasons that lack true value. They believe they are men simply because they refuse to run. The epidemic of gang violence continues to escalate in large and small communities in almost every state in the nation. This deceptive spirit has convinced men that retaliation is the answer that qualifies them as men. These wars exact a horrific toll on the aborted futures of young men. The collateral damage is equally devastating. Many young women have become caught up in this counterfeit subculture, and their futures have been dramatically affected as well. Not only are these men following distorted examples of leadership, but now young women are submitting to the same kinds of negative examples as well. These challenges abound all because men believe they are not supposed to run.

Gang violence statistics are interesting to look at because of the way in which they affect society. It is unfortunate that people seek out this type of a group in order to have somewhere to belong, as gangs are now more of a criminal organization than anything else. In the past, this was not the case, as gangs were groups of workmen. Approximately 47% of gang members are Hispanic, 31% are African American, 13% are white and 7% are Asian. This is one of the few statistics that seemingly remains fairly steady over the years regardless of the rise and fall in the other statistics about gang violence.*

Manhood must not be perceived as synonymous with fighting. Fighting has never made any male a man! In fact, when God created mankind, fighting was not one of the character traits that were mentioned. Fighting has nothing to do with a man's purpose or his identity. This is true because when God made man, there was no one to fight or anything to fight for. Everything belonged to man. Everything was created for man's benefit. He did not have to fight for what he already had dominion over. In addition, there was no enemy to fight. There was no reason to run. In contrast, man was preoccupied with fulfilling the will of the Father for his life. If there is anything a man must fight for, he must fight against his own self-will in order to obey the will of the Father.

Granted, there are times and situations faced in life where fighting seems the only viable option. Even the Father is not opposed to men defending themselves or their families. Men will find themselves in crisis situations where they must protect what the Lord has entrusted to their care. Usually these seasons of trial are not the fruit of anything the man has done. This is acutely different from participation in lifestyles or activities that promote violence. This topic must be addressed simply because a multitude of young lives hang in the balance. What does it mean to be a man, and does that have anything to do with running? Men are running, but they are running from the wrong things and for the wrong reasons. Men are running from purpose, from responsibility, and especially from accountability. Future generations lack vision and seem intimidated by

---

* Brenda Hoffman, Gang Violence Statistics: Made Manual Instructions for Life, http://www.mademan.com.

the leadership expectations placed on them. In fact, these young men are fighting for the wrong things. They are fighting for reputation, for things, for all that is temporary and nonproductive. The things for which men need to fight have been abandoned.

This deception must be exposed to the light of truth. As stated before, fighting was never an original agenda item of the Father for man. After man sinned, his fight truly began. Ever since the fall of man, both the male and female have been involved in an eternal battle. But this fight is a spiritual fight. This fight is an internal fight. In reality, man is fighting to regain his sense of identity, his sense of purpose, which was lost at the moment he chose to go his own way. In similar fashion, man lost his place of authority and has been fighting ever since to regain it. This is the real struggle for all men today. The fight has always been about men realizing they are leaders and rulers who need to take their rightful places in the Kingdom of God. They represent headship, and this must be evidenced in the home, in the church, and in the workplace. The man must regain his calling as the spiritual leader of his family. He was created to be a covering, providing for the needs of those under his responsibility. Nowhere else is warfare more evident than here. This is why it is so important for men to understand the true battle. Paul reveals the realms of this battle. He outlines the parameters for men so they understand the tactics of their foe. *For our struggle is not against flesh and blood, but against the rulers, against the authorities, against the powers of this dark world and against the spiritual forces of evil in the heavenly realms* (Ephesians 6:12). Women are not the enemy; they are the glory of man. Family is not the problem; it is the mandate of God for mankind. The family is the cornerstone of all society. No wonder the family is under attack today. It is no surprise to anyone that the man is paying the greater consequence for this dilemma. After all, he represents leadership and his responsibility is to establish order. But in contrast, the male seems to be losing ground. As a result, the family has become more vulnerable because of the absence of leadership required to provide guidance and protection.

The mentality of men is also under attack. In other words, there is a battle being raged for the way men think. For example, a few generations ago the mindset of men centered on their understanding of their responsibilities. Men were taught they were responsible for their families. Men understood they were married and held their relationship as sacred. But today's mentality has definitely changed. Too many young men today have no regard for commitment or any sense of the sanctity of marriage. In fact, far too many men have little or no respect for women. Women have been devalued in their experiences and thus the change in the way men view relationships. This becomes a battle of the mind where men's thoughts are contrary to biblical truth. Men are thinking differently about employment, commitment, relationships, and even their own identities. More men struggle with purpose because they have never been taught their value. This is a battle, and it must be fought in the spiritual realm if it is to be won. Paul penned these words:

> *For though we live in the world, we do not wage war as the world does. The weapons we fight with are not the weapons of the world. On the contrary, they have divine power to demolish strongholds. We demolish arguments and every pretention that sets itself up against the knowledge of God, and we take captive every thought to make it obedient to Christ. And we will be ready to punish every act of disobedience, once your obedience is complete.*
> —2 CORINTHIANS 10:3–6

This is the real battle! It is one that addresses the way men think. Do not underestimate this point. The Word of God is the standard by which truth is realized. When men think contrary to the truth of God's Word, they will think differently about relationships, employment, and education. When men grow up without the revelation of truth that comes from the Word of God, they will be in darkness concerning their purposes, confused about their identities, and inconsistent when it comes to their responsibilities as leaders. If there was ever an area where men need to be sharpened, it is in their thinking.

Running in the Wrong Direction

Any time a man runs in the wrong direction, he will end up in the wrong place. Men often act confused about the place in which they find themselves. However, no one arrives in any location without first making a decision about direction. It may never have been his intention to end up in the place where he is now, but he did not arrive there by accident. The Word of the Lord declares: *There is a way that appears to be right, but in the end it leads to death* (Proverbs 14:12). Direction is very important to God. He created man with a certain direction in mind. The Father wanted man to follow Him. He desired for men to walk in His ways. The Lord proved this point over and over again. When the children of Israel were freed from Egypt, they were led by the Lord through the wilderness. *By day the LORD went ahead of them in a pillar of cloud to guide them on their way and by night in a pillar of fire to give them light, so that they could travel by day or night* (Exodus 13:21). Notice God did not leave man responsible for finding his own way. The Father intentionally provided direction for man. The Lord had promised the Israelites a land flowing with milk and honey. His desire was for them to possess the land and bring it under His influence. The Israelites were to live in the land according to the ways of their God.

God wills for every man to follow Him. He wants to fulfill His purpose in every man's life. But more importantly, God yearns for every man to know His ways. Then when men are blessed and have experienced the promises of God, they will not forsake His ways. They will live according to the commandments of the Lord. Remember when the thing created by God fulfills His purpose for creating it, this brings glory to God. This is the heart of God! Man was meant to bring Him glory. However, this could only happen as a result of men following Him. The Father has never been confused about direction. In addition, He has never been confused about His purpose for man. Man was always created to follow God, but his tendency is to lose his direction.

Man, as the glory of God, has lost his direction. As a result, he continues to live beneath his privilege. Men struggle to reach their full potential. This struggle involves every aspect of a man's being. Men struggle as fathers, as husbands, and as providers for their families. Men are struggling with their identities and their purpose. How is it that men have become so lost? What explanation is there for the loss of generations of young men to hopelessness and lawlessness? Fathers have lost the ability to connect with sons. Husbands have lost the vision necessary to lead their wives. Far too many homes lack the influence of a man because he has simply lost his sense of direction. Men were never intended to abandon their families. They were not created to be in bondage unable to guide their loved ones to the truth of God's love. When did men stop following the directions provided by the Father? If men are not following the Lord, who are they following? Where are they going? No man is exempt from the need for direction. No man can lead himself and be successful. No man can affirm himself. Every man is uniquely connected to his Creator and to one another. When men understand this connection, this need for divine direction in their lives and for godly counsel from fathers, they will find their true purpose and walk in the established direction ordained for them. Without this revelation of the need for God's direction, men will continue to be lead astray following false gods and seeking after the things of this world that will never bring them fulfillment. Fulfillment can only be found in God's will for their lives.

Chapter 8

MAKING AN ARMY OF MEN

A Forgotten Art

Men have forgotten how to make things. In the past men not only made things, they were also taught the process. Men learned how to plant and to harvest. They were taught to hunt and to prepare the meat. Everyone knew how to preserve food. Men were taught to be productive, to cultivate, and to build. Men were taught responsibility. They raised livestock and understood the importance of caring for them. They understood the process. They were able to see the bigger picture. They understood their role in the organization of the family and the impact of their contribution. Children used to spend the summers with their grandparents. This was a life clinic where lessons about family and values were learned. This may have involved feeding chickens or collecting the eggs. It might have involved slopping the hogs, baling hay, or cleaning out stalls. It seemed everyone fished and hunted. This was necessary to supplement food resources. Everyone had a garden, and many of a child's initial lessons about work were developed there. No child was exempt from chores, which were assigned, and the expectations were clear: one worked before one played. Boys and girls worked alongside their fathers and mothers. Girls learned to cook and to sew. Boys learned the importance of family and the responsibility of manhood. Children were taught the value of relationships. Little things were given priority. Life was not about an abundance of possessions, but rather an appreciation for the things one had and the fact that basic needs were always met. If someone needed something, they were taught to work for it. Sacrifice was the order of the day, and patience was truly a virtue.

Men have forgotten how to make things. They struggle because they have no longer been taught these basic lessons of life. Each succeeding generation has lost appreciation for the process. Men are no longer content with anything, and children have lost the sense of appreciation for the things they already have. In fact, things don't last long anymore. Everything is being upgraded, and this has created an atmosphere of the temporary. No one really expects anything to last long anymore. The mentality today is to anticipate the next and newest model when in reality, the previous model still works. This has led to a perception that there is little or no value in anything old. This subtle invasion upon the hearts and minds of generations has subconsciously altered the moral standards of life. For example, marriages don't last long today in contrast to those of the past two generations. The tragedy is that no one questions why, for too many people have just accepted divorce as norm. Remember, nothing is expected to last long. There is little value in anything old and, above all, respect for the process has been severely compromised. Fathers are struggling to impart the disciplines of responsibility, accountability, integrity, and perseverance to their sons and daughters. Men must know they still have to work for their relationships, their dreams, and their goals. Men still have to be taught that vision demands commitment and success requires sacrifice. The temporary mentality and approach to life is not sufficient when attempting to establish and build a life today. In short, men must be taught again how to make things. Every son must know how to build a relationship and sustain a marriage. Each boy must be taught the value of the process so he realizes what it means to cultivate and build a family. Every man will be tested in the disciplines of life. Can he handle the scrutiny of accountability? Has he learned the lessons of manhood, and does he appreciate and respect the process? When he looks back on his life, to whom will he give the credit for making him a man?

God made everything. Nothing exists today apart from God. This is true because the creator of a thing is responsible for what he created. Parents are to be responsible for the children they produce. It is difficult to comprehend a parent who abandons his or her child, a father who deserts his family, or a man who denies his responsibility. God has always taken care of His creation. Our heavenly Father has never turned His back on anything He created. God is never content to leave things in a formless or empty state. The Father will never allow darkness to cover His creation, because darkness is not representative of His nature. God is the Creator, the Originator, and the Source of all things. Our heavenly Father has always had a vision for man. He sees man fulfilling His created purpose for him. His heart's desire is to see men mature in His will for them. The Father is not content for man to remain immature, in darkness, and miss His plan for them.

Each man represents a family. This is not only his potential, but also his purpose. Men must understand they have seed in them, and seed represents the ability to reproduce one's self. This gift must not be taken lightly or treated as insignificant. A mature man understands he was created to be a father, but becoming a father is the result of raising children to the place where they are able to duplicate the process. Each man must accept the responsibility to lead his family in godliness. In order to accomplish this, every man must know the Lord. It is virtually impossible for a man to find his purpose apart from his heavenly Father. This is the fundamental rationale for why natural fathers are so necessary. Whether they realize it or not, their children find their purpose in them because they are their source. Fathers represent the source when it comes to the family. Identity is tied to the father. When men realize their need for a heavenly Father, they can discover their purposes.

The man represents the glory of God. He is to be the premier representation of the Father in the earth. Wives are praying for their husbands to lead. However, leadership must be comprehensive. Men were created to lead their families spiritually, economically, emotionally, as well as physically. Although they are to be providers, they must also provide vision for the marriage and the home. As prophets and priests, men are to speak life into their families and provide direction and the nurturing necessary to make their vision a reality in the lives of those for whom they provide covering. Children must take ownership of the vision of the house. The vision of the house must become the standard of their lives. This is accomplished when children become adults and implement these same standards in their homes. Fathers and mothers are to equip sons and daughters so they are able to operate their lives independent of their parents. When parents provide nurture and discipline, they will produce mature and responsible young people who are able to endure the process and respect the role they are called to play. This need and calling to make things, to reproduce and replenish the earth, must be taken seriously. It will never be appreciated if young men and young women continue to live superficially, disrespecting God's will for their lives. Future generations must be taught that life is about process. It is one thing to be born; it's another thing to become responsible. It is one thing to get married; it is altogether something else to be committed to making that marriage last. The challenges of life demand men who are committed to the process remaining in place until the purpose has been fulfilled. Men cannot be allowed to continue in life with a misunderstanding of what life is really all about.

Rediscovering the Act of Making Things

There is always the difference between the moment and the process. Things are birthed in moments, but to fulfill purpose requires a process. Joseph dreamed a dream in moments, yet the fulfillment of his dream demanded a lifetime. Generations past understood the process. There was an appreciation for the process because they understood it brought maturity. Today's generation knows little about the process. They want everything immediately. In fact, today's generation seems to pursue ways of bypassing the process. The end result is an immature generation who struggles with purpose. Purpose is best understood in the light of process. Purpose is generally fulfilled when the process is appreciated. Men must realize their role is to lead their families through the seasons of life. The man must accept the responsibility to impart to his family the necessity of going through the process. Wives and children expect husbands and fathers to lead them. They are quite disappointed when fathers fail to provide the leadership they so desperately need.

God the Father has always been committed to the process. The Lord has never been impressed by the temporary or by what is immediately visible. In contrast, the world in which men live has placed all the attention on appearance. Mankind has become so consumed with appearance that they are easily conformed to the ways of this world. In fact, the world attempts to redefine everything according to its standards. This redefining of reality has had a damaging impact on generations of men. They have been bombarded by false expectations, twisted definitions of manhood, warped ideas of responsibility, and a complete abandonment of any accountability. Generations of men have bought into the deception that true manhood is about the temporary accumulation of things. This generation of men defines success as the attainment of power based on status or bling and the ever-present myth that life is about women, wealth, and happiness. Many men believe that money and things are what life is all about. In addition, many men have become addicted to power. Power represents their ability to be in control. However, many of these same men have never been taught the will of God concerning them. As a result, these men end up trying to control other people while being controlled by things.

Men have forgotten how to make things. Mankind was created to be like God, mirroring His character and walking in His ways. In other words, mankind was given authority to operate as God operates. God moves with creative power according to His divine plan. He is committed to see His purpose fulfilled in the earth through men. He created man to share this divine venture with Him. This is why the Father shared authority with man. Mankind was created to share in God's glorious manifestation of His Kingdom in the earth. The Father made everything and shared this ability with men. Man, as a leader, is to share with others what the Father has shared with him. Adam had this responsibility. He was to share with Eve the truths the Father had shared with him. In similar fashion, men are to share God's truths with their families. This is a huge responsibility, and the enemy is equally committed to keeping men in darkness.

This is the reason why so many men fail to realize their spiritual responsibility when it comes to leading their families. This is why church attendance is not the man's greatest priority. He would rather send his family and remain at home as if that were an example of leadership. The problem with this deception is that it manifests in other areas of his life. If he fails to lead spiritually, he may also fail to lead emotionally, becoming a quiet partner in the marriage relationship. He may fail to lead financially, denying his role to provide for his family. This is not a problem traced to circumstance but a matter of the heart. This is a part of who a man is. He should innately feel a sense of responsibility to provide for his family. At one point in time this was considered a mark of manhood. It appears manhood today is defined in other ways. God's purpose for creating men must not be lost to deception, darkness, or the pervasive influence of culture. Rather, fathers must return to the old foundations and rebuild the walls representing manhood. Sons must once again understand fatherhood in light of their heavenly Father's purpose for creating them.

The Bible reveals much about the character of God in light of making things. *"I am the Alpha and the Omega," says the Lord God, "who is, and who was, and who is to come, the Almighty"* (Revelation 1:8). God never speaks of faithfulness only in terms of the beginning of a thing. The fulfillment of anything made is never found in its origin but in its completion. This is why process is imperative with God. He created man with destiny in mind. Man was made to become something and then to accomplish something else. If each man is to know the will of God, he must submit to the entire plan of God for his life. He must patiently trust the Father to complete in him what He has started. Each man must realize he is called to represent God who is always faithful to finish what He begins. This revelation should transform the mentality of men.

Young men must remember that others will depend on them to finish the race of life they have begun. How many wives have prayed for a husband to be committed to their relationship? Countless children have imagined what a faithful father would look like in their lives. How many sons have grown up promising themselves they will not be like their own fathers? This is because too many men have grown up with the perception that simply birthing something, whether a child or a marriage, is the fulfillment of purpose. This deception must be exposed. True leadership demands more. Once a child is born, the role of a father makes that man significant. His responsibility is now greater than ever before. When a man commits to a woman in holy matrimony, it is just the beginning. The wife is now looking to her husband to keep his vows in a lifelong commitment to their marriage and ultimately to their future family. The true measure of a man's commitment does not take place in a moment but is only realized by his submission to the process.

What the Father Has to Work With

Whenever you make something, you need to think about what you are going to use to make it. Usually when something is being made, the attention is on the finished product. However, it is also important to think about the purpose for which the finished product was made. *David left Gath and escaped to the cave of Adullam. When his brothers and his father's household heard about it, they went down to him there* (1 Samuel 22:1). Notice it was David's family who came to him. Remember David was the youngest of all his brothers, and he also was the one who had been overlooked as a legitimate candidate for kingship. It is obvious that what his family failed to see before they saw now. Something had happened that provided them literal insight to see David as king even though he had not ascended to the throne of Israel. In addition, *all those who were in distress or in debt or discontented gathered around him, and he became their commander* (1 Samuel 22:2). This verse refers to men who were struggling to fulfill their destiny. Many men today are struggling to fulfill their purpose as well.

When men struggle to fulfill their created purpose, it implies that something is missing. God did not create man to miss his purpose or to fail to accomplish His will. These men came to David. In other words, their destiny or ability to accomplish their purpose was tied to David. In the midst of all their struggles, God was directing them to His answer for them. Men must understand their ability to become mature men is always tied to other men. This is what is meant by the revelation: *As iron sharpens iron, so one person sharpens another* (Proverbs 27:17). God created man as a leader. The men of Israel came to David because they needed a leader. They came to David, and he became their leader. God's will is that all men discover their calling to lead. In the same way God provides leadership for His creation, men are to provide leadership for those under their covering. God is looking for leaders, and when He discovers them He will always send others to them.

David had to discover the leader in himself. He had been anointed as the next king in Israel. David had to believe in himself, and this meant he had to deal with the obvious rejection from his natural father. He was not even considered as a possibility for kingship. It was as if he was an afterthought. He also had to deal with his brothers. It was not easy being the baby in the family. He was looked down on by them, and in their eyes, he would never be able to compete on their level. And to add insult to injury, he had been anointed to be king in their presence. Even after they witnessed this moment, they did not believe it would become a reality. David had to believe in himself in spite of all those who did not believe in him. This situation was further complicated by King Saul who determined to negate any possibility of David becoming king anywhere. But in spite of all these challenges, God was determined to make an army of men. This meant David must become a leader.

A Surprise from on High

Every man must believe in himself. A man believing in himself is more complicated than it appears. It is not easy being a man in today's environment. Men have always been under natural and spiritual attack by the enemy. Satan was an archangel created to worship God. His responsibility was to recognize the Lordship of the Father and give Him the glory due His name. But somewhere along the way, Satan became twisted and lost sight of who God truly was. He desired to take God's place by coveting the Father's praise and glory for himself. His intent was exposed, and he was cast from the presence of the Lord for eternity. God created man in His image and likeness and declared that man was His glory. Mankind was created as the jewel of the Father's creation and alone had the awesome responsibility of responding to God's love. This is the reason why the Father sent His Son into the world to die for man's sins. Love is the foundation of all things, especially worship. Man was created to love God and, as a result, to worship Him. True worship is only the result of a consuming love for a God who is worthy of all man's praise and adoration.

Men need to know how much they are loved by God. Furthermore, they must be taught about their roles as leaders who are destined to lead their families in loving and worshipping the Lord. Men are called to exemplify the Father's love to their wives and children. Their love for God is the foundation for everything they do for those they love. When men learn to lead, it is preparation for their calling to reign. But just like David, before men can reign, they must first become leaders. It is true they will learn leadership through their experiences, but most of their leadership training is found in the heart of their Creator revealed to them in His Word. The Father has spent lifetimes attempting to reveal to men their roles of leadership and the expectations He has of them. David was no exception. He, too, had to grasp the Father's divine plan for his life and learn to fulfill his calling by loving and worshipping God. Only God can reveal to each man His deep love for him. God alone must draw men to Himself, exposing them to the greater role they are to play in this life.

Learning to love and worship God is a process requiring obedience and commitment. The Father desires that each person would live his or her life as a sacrifice of worship. It is easy to love the world and the things of the world, and more and more men have become consumed with the systems of this world. But more importantly, men seem to be losing sight of the created order entrusted to them. Whenever God wants to accomplish something, He looks for a man He can use to fulfill His will. *The LORD said, "I have indeed seen the misery of my people in Egypt. I have heard them crying out because of their slave drivers, and I am concerned about their suffering. So I have come down to rescue them from the hand of the Egyptians and to bring them up out of that land into a good and a spacious land, a land flowing with milk and honey"* (Exodus 3:7–8a). If one were to read these verses literally, the conclusion might be that God

Himself had come to earth to take care of His people. But men must be reminded they are leaders. As such, they are prime candidates to be called upon by the Father. God simply needs to reveal Himself to men so He can communicate His plan to them.

And now the cry of the Israelites has reached me, and I have seen the way the Egyptians are oppressing them. So now, go. I am sending you to Pharaoh to bring my people the Israelites out of Egypt (Exodus 3:9–10). God always intended to send men to address the problems of His people. Moses seemed content to allow God to go, to perform all that He had declared to him. But then the Father revealed that Moses was a part of His plan. Again this is God's will, and He has not changed His strategy. The children of Israel were in trouble and required immediate attention. The Lord understood this and commanded Moses to go. Moses was to go right then. There was no putting it off. God had heard His children's cries, seen their oppression, and was determined to deliver them. The people's need for deliverance is greater today, as this generation has been exposed to spiritual warfare on levels unparalleled before. Men must not be surprised by the call of the Father to bring deliverance to their families and their communities. God is calling men to go now. Men must move immediately if they are to restore order, redeem the time, and see their seed delivered from the oppression of the rulers of this world.

It is obvious God believed in Moses. The Father saw something in Moses He could use. The Lord simply had to convince Moses he was the right person for the job. This need remains today. Every man must be convinced he is the right person for the task. Like Moses, so many men are still raising the same doubts today. *"What if they do not believe me or listen to me and say, 'The LORD did not appear to you'?"* (Exodus 4:1). Many men, when trying to provide vision for their homes, ask this same question. How do men convince their families the Lord has really spoken to them? The answer is by living and exercising the authority given to them by God. If men are unsure of their own authority, everyone else will surely doubt it. But when men walk boldly and consistently in their roles, others can only respect them. Moses had to come to a place of maturity in his life, and he realized his authority and walked boldly in it. Regardless of self-imposed limitations or those placed on men by others, men must believe they are leaders who are destined to become kings.

Many men have never led. They have never been in positions of leadership where they have been respected. Furthermore, they have had no examples to teach them. They have not witnessed the trials and tribulations of the generations before them. And yet in their present lives, they are facing conditions requiring a different kind of leadership than that to which they are accustomed. No challenge is without cause. The children of Israel found themselves again in trouble with their enemies. The reason was also a familiar one.

> When the Israelites cried to the LORD because of Midian, he sent them a prophet who said, "This is what the LORD, the God of Israel, says: I brought you up out of Egypt, out of the land of slavery.... I delivered you from the hand of all your oppressors; I drove them before you and gave you their land. I said to you, 'I am the LORD your God; do not worship the gods of the Amorites, in whose land you live.' But you have not listened to me."
> —JUDGES 6:7–10

Israel's disobedience permitted their enemies access to them. Sometimes God will allow your enemy access to you because of your disobedience. The Father's expectations are clear, and when men choose to walk contrary to His will, they place themselves in a vulnerable position. It is evident the children of Israel did not heed the word of the Lord. As a result, they found themselves under the oppression of the Midianites. What happens when a people are oppressed? Usually they cry unto the Lord. God is committed to man's deliverance from oppression. This was ultimately demonstrated by the life of Jesus Christ. Luke testified concerning Jesus: *You know what has happened throughout the province of Judea, beginning in Galilee after the baptism that John preached—how God anointed Jesus of Nazareth with the Holy Spirit and power, and how he went around doing good and healing all who were under the power of the devil, because God was with him* (Acts 10:37–38). It was never God's will for His creation to live under Satan's power. God created man to walk in dominion.

God is never content to leave mankind under oppression. He will always be attentive to the cries of His people when they are being mistreated by their enemies. We have already discovered that God always looks for men He can use in order to deliver His people. If God is to build an army, He must first identify and prepare leaders. God is looking for leaders today. The question is whether He can find men who are willing to be prepared. The Father is as serious about the preparation of the leaders as He is about the deliverance of His people. Preparation involves a process necessary to transform the leader while redeeming a people. The challenge is not always whether the Lord can find a man, but whether the man is willing to go through the process.

The children of Israel found themselves under the torment of their enemies. Because their oppression was so heavy, they were forced to live in mountain cliffs and caves. They were constantly in hiding from their oppressors. Their bondage drove them to cry out to the Lord who, in response to their cries, went seeking for a man. *The angel of the LORD came and sat down under the oak in Ophrah that belonged to Joash the Abiezrite, where his son Gideon was threshing wheat in a winepress to keep it from the Midianites. When the angel of the LORD appeared to Gideon, he said, "The LORD is with you, mighty warrior"* (Judges 6:11–12). Gideon was no exception to the plight in which the people of God had found themselves. In addition, he served as a fitting example of a man who had lost touch with his God-given authority. He was threshing wheat in a winepress. Apparently the Midianites, Amalekites, and other eastern people were systematically invading the country of the Israelites, destroying everything they produced. Those enemies destroyed their crops and slaughtered their livestock. One thing is absolutely sure: Israel was under oppression. *They came up with their livestock and their tents like swarms of locusts. It was impossible to count them or their camels; they invaded the land to ravage it. Midian so impoverished the Israelites that they cried out to the LORD for help* (Judges 6:5–6). The intention of these enemies was clear. They meant to reduce the people of God to literal starvation. They not only wanted to destroy every means of survival, but they also cared nothing for the lives of the people. Thus the people had been reduced to hiding with no leader in sight.

Gideon was afraid like everyone else. In fact, he was hiding from his enemies, attempting to preserve what little substance he had remaining. He was threshing wheat in a wine press with the hope he would not be discovered. This potentially represented the last portion of food available to him and his father's house. But under those circumstances, he was visited by an angel of the Lord. It was in this context, and under those conditions, that he was singled out by God as someone with potential. It is amazing whom God will visit to do His will. Most men would question God's judgment at the very least. God knows what He is doing. Gideon may not have looked like a mighty warrior, but he possessed the potential to lead. In reality, the process had already started, and he appeared to be in the middle of it. The angel of the Lord greeted Gideon and called him a mighty warrior. This may surprise those who read it because Gideon was in hiding. He was threshing wheat in a wine press. How could he be identified as a mighty warrior? But this was how God saw Gideon. The Lord saw Gideon through His eyes, not as Gideon saw himself.

God has singled out every man as a person with potential. Each man is called to do great exploits for the Lord. He may be in hiding or intimidated by his enemies, but God sees him as a mighty warrior. Thank God He sees each man through His own eyes. *When the angel of the LORD appeared to Gideon, he said, "The LORD is with you, mighty warrior"* (Judges 6:12). This even took Gideon by surprise. Like most men, Gideon saw himself in light of his circumstances. Gideon had limited himself according to his situation. His perception of his potential had been dramatically altered by his limitations. Many men discount their potential because of the struggles they go through. Others forsake their authority, concluding there is little if anything they can do in light of the challenges before them. Men must be convinced their authority is God-given. Their call to walk in dominion is never based on circumstance. As a result, men must realize they are not limited regardless of the crisis in which they find themselves.

"Pardon me, my lord," Gideon replied, "but if the LORD is with us, why has all this happened to us? Where are all His wonders that our ancestors told us about when they said, 'Did not the LORD bring us up out of Egypt?' But now the LORD has abandoned us and given us into the hand of Midian" (Judges 6:13). These are legitimate questions. Every man asks these questions at some point in his life. Why has this happened to us? Where is

the God our fathers talked about? Gideon had heard of the mighty acts of God, but his immediate situation had not changed. As far as he was concerned, the Lord had forsaken Israel. They were suffering under the oppression of the Midianites. The angel responded to Gideon as if he did not hear his complaint or was not concerned with his circumstances. *The LORD turned to him and said, "Go in the strength you have and save Israel out of Midian's hand. Am I not sending you?"* (Judges 6:14). Most men in this position would wonder what the angel of the Lord was talking about. Gideon was told to go in his strength. The problem was he did not believe he had strength. Gideon responded by saying: *"Pardon me, my lord…but how can I save Israel? My clan is the weakest in Manasseh, and I am the least in my family"* (Judges 6:15).

Men must be careful how they live. Men cannot afford to give up because of their circumstances. There are always others who are depending on them. There will be those who look to them for leadership, protection, and for faith. Be reminded that if you are the least in your family, you are a prime candidate to be chosen by the Lord. The Lord simply desires to use ordinary men to do extraordinary things. The Lord was convinced of Gideon's potential, but Gideon still needed to be convinced. The Lord literally declared the outcome of this conflict. He confirmed to Gideon that He would be with him, and his enemies would be defeated. Every man must understand he can do all things if God is present with him. Each man's focus must shift from his present circumstances to the promises of God.

When Men Need a Sign

Sometimes it is difficult for men to see past their present circumstances. The pressures of responsibilities can be overwhelming. Furthermore, there are no short cuts in life. Each person must submit to the process. It is a necessary part of life that results in personal growth and wisdom. The children of Israel were involved in the process. They had failed to heed the Word of the Lord and were now suffering the consequences. The process had taken its toll on them. God had appeared to Gideon and assured him He had not forsaken His people. Gideon represented another generation who had not witnessed the miracles of God. They had been told about the awesome exploits God had worked on behalf of His people, but it appeared those experiences were a thing of the past. The children of Israel had strayed away from the will of the Father.

> *Joshua, son of Nun, the servant of the LORD, died at the age of a hundred and ten. After that whole generation had been gathered to their ancestors, another generation grew up who knew neither the LORD nor what He had done for Israel. Then the Israelites did evil in the eyes of the LORD and served the Baals.*
> —JOSHUA 2:8, 10–11

God again must reveal Himself to His people. Gideon belonged to this new generation. This is the reason he was bewildered about the God of Israel. He had been told about Him but had never known Him. Now the God he had heard about appeared to him. Not only had He appeared to him, but He also revealed His will to deliver His people and destroy the Midianites. Only one thing was surprising—God wanted to use him. The Lord had given him His Word and declared He would be with him. God was looking for a leader and someone He could use to lead when everyone else was hiding. God again was intent on making an army of men. The only thing He needed was a leader.

Today we have a generation of men who have grown up without any real revelation of the Lord. Like those before them, they have been told about the goodness of the Lord, His mighty acts, His power and His promises. But many young men today have grown up outside the church. Some of them have never been involved in a church because this was not a priority in their homes. Still others did not have an example. The reality today is many of these young men lack any understanding of their God-given, God-ordained roles in the earth. It is no small wonder that many of these men lack vision for the future or understanding for the present. They have not been given the insight necessary to possess a mature picture of life as a man. Therefore, no one should be surprised by their confusion and lack of motivation. When men are blind to who they are, have no idea of their purpose, nor are aware of their measure of rule or their sphere of influence, they will go into hiding. These men will succumb to their circumstances and be limited by their conditions. They will become prey to the enemies of their times, not realizing they are being conformed to the patterns and mentality of the world in which they live. Like Gideon, they will begin to doubt their own futures while giving up subconsciously on the God of their fathers. It is easy to lose your way when you are already lost. Young men today have accepted their conditions, their situations, their circumstances as normal. They view themselves as the victims of their environment, destined always to be enslaved by it. This is quickly becoming a hopeless generation. Far too many men see no alternatives to their predicament. Like Gideon, they have decided to hide, grinding wheat in the wine presses of life.

Gideon had come to this point in his own life. He witnessed personally the plunder of his own nation by the Midianites. He was living proof that times were hard, and even the alternatives for his family were limited.

Israel had been reduced to surviving. Gideon knew this was not God's will for his life. He somehow understood his purpose was so much greater than his present situation. In reality, he was reaching out to God, the God of his fathers. He had questions for which he wanted answers. The same thing is true even now. Men have questions and feel like there is no place they can go to find the answers. They are wondering where God is. Can He really make a difference in their lives? Does He really exist? If He does, where is He? Men want more! There is more to life than just being successful. According to the standards of this life, we are reminded it is possible to become successful, to become satisfied with the things of this world, and yet not be fulfilled.

Men must be taught the truth about their existence. God wants men to be blessed. But even God wants more from men. He wants men to be witnesses of fatherhood. Men must know they are blessed to be a blessing. This is the responsibility of a father, to bless his own children. True fulfillment involves completing the task begun. For example, raising a child to adulthood brings fulfillment. Fathers must invest in their sons' and daughters' fulfillment. A husband remaining committed to his wife for a lifetime is truly fulfillment. When men realize they have weathered the storms of life and provided leadership and direction for their families, this is fulfillment. God has always wanted more from men. It was never God's will for men to quit, to give up in hopelessness. The Father never intended for men to become confused about their calling to lead or their responsibility to provide. He wants men to lead spiritually, to provide a covering for their wives and children. God has always wanted men to respect their identity, pursue their purpose, and walk in their authority. This can only happen when men know God. This is why God reveals

Himself to men. This is why God revealed Himself to Gideon. Finally, this is why God calls men to leadership. Sometimes it just takes a sign.

Gideon, though surprised, was not confused. He was now fully aware of the Father's plan and his role in it. He had presented all his excuses only to find none of them would suffice. His back was against the wall one more time. What do you do when you're face-to-face with the living God? Like Gideon, you ask for a sign. *Gideon replied, "If now I have found favor in your eyes, give me a sign that it is really you talking to me"* (Judges 6:17). This is a very important place for a man to find himself. Men must know it is God who is speaking to them. Before men can become leaders, this question must always be answered. Gideon bought a sacrifice to the Lord and then was told to tear down his own father's altar to Baal, an idol god. What is amazing is the fact Gideon did not do this alone. The record shows that *Gideon took ten of his servants and did as the LORD told him. But because he was afraid of his family and the townspeople, he did it at night rather than in the daytime* (Judges 6:27). The fact Gideon was afraid or did what he did at night is not the revelation. The true revelation is Gideon had become a leader. He had gone from hiding to leading. Something happened to Gideon that moved him past his fears of family or neighbors. He now was committed to God. He had found his purpose. Men will always follow a man who has found his true purpose. Think about it: no one wants to follow a man in hiding. No one will follow a man who lacks vision. But when men find their purpose and begin to walk in it, others will follow.

What Gideon did caused uproar among the people of his own town. He had disrespected their gods. They wanted him dead. But it was his own father who stood up for him and defied the demands of the crowd.

> *But Joash replied to the hostile crowd around him, "Are you going to plead Baal's cause? Are you trying to save him? Whoever fights for him shall be put to death by morning! If Baal really is a god, he can defend himself when someone breaks down his altar." So because Gideon broke down Baal's altar, they gave him the name Jerub-Baal that day saying, "Let Baal contend with him."*
>
> —Judges 6:31–32

Notice Gideon had gone from being a leader in the eyes of his servants to being a leader in the eyes of his city. This one act of obedience had not only transformed Gideon but also his entire city. It is important to note it was his father who stood between him and the crowd. This might be considered an example of our heavenly Father. He also stands in the gap between mankind and the spiritual forces of wickedness in this world. When the enemy rears up and demands men's deaths, God intervenes by letting the enemy know he must fight his own battles. The enemy cannot be allowed to use men to do his dirty work. This has been a trick of the enemy from the beginning. If the truth were told, the enemy needs men's help. This is why James wrote: *Resist the devil and he will flee from you* (James 4:7). The enemy must be exposed for the false god that he is. He has no justified power against men. The only power he has is the power given to him by men. God, however, wants to empower men to defeat the enemy in their own lives and then fight for the freedom of others.

How does the story end? The Midianites were not leaving on their own. The children of Israel would find no deliverance without a deliverer. In every situation where people are oppressed, God must raise up a leader, someone men can follow. This was the case with Gideon and Israel at this time. God caused men to follow Gideon as a leader, but He wanted Gideon to be mindful of who the true leader really was. Gideon had finally accepted the fact he was called by God to lead. He had placed fleeces before God, and the Lord had responded. Gideon had become a leader to his own people.

> *Early in the morning, Jerub-Baal (that is, Gideon) and all his men camped at the spring of Harod. The camp of Midian was north of them in the valley near the hill of Moreh. The LORD said to Gideon, "You have too many men. I cannot deliver Midian into their hands, or Israel would boast against me, 'My own strength has saved me.' Now announce now to the army, 'Anyone who trembles with fear may turn back and leave Mount Gilead.'"*
>
> —JUDGES 7:1–3

As a result, some 22,000 men left while 10,000 remained. Notice that God revealed to Gideon His position concerning the mentality of the people of Israel. The Lord had no intention of giving the people any opportunity to boast. He did not want them confused about the source of their impending victory. He clearly communicated that there were too many men with Gideon. Gideon announced that if anyone was fearful, he could leave with no questions asked. The text reveals that 22,000 men left. Surely Gideon must have been impacted by this desertion. He had just come into leadership. He was still trying to adjust to his newfound role. He somehow had gone from hiding to now leading a mighty army of men. He was strategically positioned to be recognized by everyone. But now he had just witnessed 22,000 men abandon his army. God had revealed to him that he had too many men. He had continued by sharing His rationale: He did not want Israel to think they won this battle in their own strength. But what was God teaching Gideon? There are always lessons for the leader to learn.

First, the Lord wanted Gideon's focus to be on Him. Every leader must trust God regardless of the situation in which he is leading. Next, the leader must operate in faith. Each man must realize he does not control the outcome of the battle. God reinforced this lesson by decreasing the visible army supporting Gideon. In other words, the outcome or victory is never based on the number of men a leader may have with him. In fact, God reduced the number of men Gideon had fighting with him a second time, yet the enemy's army was not any smaller. The Lord wants the leader to learn to hear and obey His voice. Men will hear many voices when their visible resources are diminished and their challenges remain the same. Gideon had to learn to trust in the voice of the Lord. *The LORD said to Gideon, "With the three hundred men that lapped I will save you and give the Midianites into your hands"* (Judges 7:7). Each man must realize God will not fail him. He may not provide deliverance according to the leader's expectations, but He will always deliver. When men need a sign, God will give them His Word. God's Word is the sign of His promise and His unfailing love. May every man live his life according to the Father's Word.

Chapter 9

THE NECESSITY
OF LEADERSHIP

*A Moment That Demands
Leadership*

Man has always been a leader in the mind of God. The male man was uniquely positioned to represent his Creator by providing leadership for others. God recognized that man (mankind) needed leadership from the very beginning. Even in the Garden of Eden—a perfect environment—man was not left to himself. God has always provided man with leadership. He gave him directions and revealed to him his purpose. He set boundaries for man and clarified His expectations. God never left man to chance. He wanted the first man, Adam, to understand who his Father was. Put another way, He wanted Adam to know he was created to be a father as well. Man was created to follow God. He was created in the Father's likeness and in His image. He was made to lead. Mankind would only realize the Father's will by following Him. Whenever men decide to follow their own wills or the will of others, they will always forfeit leadership. Every man must understand leadership was not given to him independent of his Creator. In other words, leadership is always given with purpose, yet the recipient of leadership is never the source of purpose. Purpose is always found in the heart of the Creator. When men comprehend this truth, they realize there is a correct way to lead. Leadership is necessary, but godly leadership is critical.

God is naturally a leader. One might say He is a leader because He's God. This assumption is true. He is the beginning and the end of all things. He knows where everything was meant to be. He also knows what every person was created to become. All created things have their place. Fish find their place in water. Birds are at home in the air. Plants can draw their life from either the earth or the sea. The same is true with animals. Some are more at home on land while others have adapted more to water. But in every case there is a specific locale for every created thing. When God created man, his purpose transcended a specific location. Mankind was to replenish the earth. In other words, man was to be everywhere in the earth. Man was given dominion over all creation. God created him with the specific purpose of becoming a leader. This is why God placed man in the Garden of Eden. Once there, the Lord communicated to Adam his responsibilities. He was to dress the garden and take care of it. He was the overseer of all the fish and birds, the gardener of every plant, and the caretaker of every living creature on the earth. In reality, God intended for man to take care of all creation regardless of where it was located in the earth. Man was created to provide leadership.

The Garden of Eden served as a testing place to develop man's leadership ability. Men must be reminded just because they were created to lead does not mean they know how to lead. These skills must be learned. Leadership must not only be taught, but it must also be tested. Every boy born in this earth is a leader. This is his purpose. This remains God's plan for him. God was intentional about this, so He put the seed in the man. This implies that in every boy there is a father. This infers in every boy there is a family. This could mean in every boy there is a potential husband, provider, or protector. But even though all of these possibilities are in the boy, he does not know how to be any of them yet. Therefore his life in this earth becomes the testing place to see if he will become what he was always created to be. His options are few. He cannot remain a boy even if he wants to. He cannot stay a child even if his mother wants him to. He must grow up in spite of his shortcomings or limitations. He will become a man physically even if he fails to become one spiritually, emotionally, or mentally.

Men cannot escape manhood. They must be taught what it means to be a man before they can fulfill the expectations of manhood. This is one of the reasons why God created man male and female and gave them dominion. He commanded them to replenish the earth but then left the woman in the man. Why did the Father do this? It might be because the man's leadership capacity had never been tested. It could have been because until then, the man had no knowledge of leadership and needed both an example and a teacher. Discernment will reveal that God took this responsibility on Himself. Who better could teach Adam about leadership? What better example could Adam have found? Who else knew more about being a father? Who understood the intricacies of being a husband more than God? History has proven there is no better provider than the Lord.

God taught Adam, the adult male, the complexities of leadership. He put him over the entire garden. He required of him to name every living creature. He taught him the boundaries of leadership. He let him know that leadership had responsibilities and that there were consequences for failing to follow his Creator's will. In other words, God was teaching Adam that he was responsible for others. God wanted this point to be clear. As a man, life is not about you and you alone. Innate in manhood is the responsibility for others. Men are always responsible for someone other than themselves. This is the reason why the man must provide covering for his wife and children. This is also the rationale why the man is the head of his house. This is also the reason why women take the man's last name in marriage. This is why fathers are supposed to give their daughters away in marriage to another man. Men were created to cover.

Adam was trained by God Himself. He was taught both the will and the ways of God. A true leader must also know God's ways. This leader will possess a heart after God even in the face of his own limitations. He will yearn for the Father's will to be completed in him. While Adam was naming the animals, he realized he could not fulfill manhood because something was missing in his own existence. This was no small revelation for Adam. When men understand the ways of God, then God can entrust to them what was missing. Eve was always in Adam, but he must be prepared to provide leadership for her. This is not to imply the confused perception of the world today—that men are to lord authority over women. In contrast, this simply means men must be taught the responsibility to provide covering for their wives and children.

Men do this naturally. Most every brother will protect his sister. Sons will defy even their own fathers if they sense their mother is being threatened. Men were always meant to be fathers, and as such, they are protectors. Adam's eyes were opened, and he realized there was no one who fit him. For the first time in his life, he concluded he needed help to complete the will of God for his life. Each man must realize his own need for a wife. She was created to make him complete. The woman was made in order for mankind to fulfill God's will. Man was never meant to be alone. Genesis 3:8 reveals: *Then the man and his wife heard the sound of the* Lord *God as he was walking in the garden in the cool of the day, and they hid from the* Lord *God among the trees of the garden.* Of course, the context of this verse occurs after the fall of man. Because they had sinned, they now hid themselves from God. One might safely assume this was not the first time God appeared to man in the garden even though it was the first time they hid. It is highly possible God had appeared in the garden and walked with Adam on numerous occasions. It is also reasonable to assume Adam had no reason to hide from the Lord before this moment. In this context, the Father was the Leader. He was teaching Adam how to lead. God was aware of His plan all along. He meant for the adult male to lead. God always meant to present the woman to the man. The Father was preparing the man because the woman would be his greatest test of leadership. This is why leadership in the home has become so confusing. Men have forgotten their call to lead while women have forsaken their call to follow. Husbands have abandoned the responsibility to provide vision and covering while wives have determined to be their own covering, pursuing their own visions. Adam found himself with his wife, hiding from the Lord, all because he had failed to lead and she had failed to follow.

No one in the home or the church talks about this much today. In fact this struggle between men and women, husbands and wives, has not been addressed much at all. Regardless, this tension is a reality that must be exposed and then confronted. God's response to both Adam and Eve, as a result of their sin, carries eternal weight even in this present time. Men can be so easily swayed by women. In the context of marriage, this is complicated even more because the man's nature is to cover and provide for his wife. Women must be careful not to manipulate their husbands. In other words, wives must not use their influence in ways contrary to the vision of their home. In an ideal situation, there is a vision in the house to which everyone is committed. Having a vision, a short and long-term plan, is critical. This plan requires focus and will prevent division in the home.

Notice again the Father's response to the woman: *Then the LORD God said to the woman, "What is this you have done?"* (Genesis 3:13). In this particular case, Eve had acted independently of her husband. She obviously struggled with having to be totally dependent on him. This is still true today. Women struggle with having to be dependent on men. In the context of relationships, daughters are dependent on fathers and wives are dependent on husbands. Although many natural variables have changed over time, the spiritual principle remains the same. The woman was not created to lead the man. Many struggle today with this concept. When Eve took the leadership position independent of her husband, order was compromised. Ultimately the authority of mankind was lost to the enemy. Thus we see the first man and woman hiding among the trees they were created to exercise authority over. Unfortunately this confusion still exists today. This is the reason for the absentee father, the unbridled divorce rate among both believers and non-believers, and the chaos of generations who struggle with their own sense of identity and self-worth. The lines have shifted. What Eve did resulted in spiritual division. This joint act by the first man and woman separated them from the presence of the Father and began a perpetual battle for leadership in the home. Regardless of the outcome, a house divided against itself cannot stand!

Man has a more critical role to play in this scenario. His failure carries more weight because he has more responsibility. The adult male was created with divine purpose. God taught Adam these responsibilities. He was responsible to dress and keep the garden, to work it and take care of it. His initial responsibility was to provide covering by protecting the environment in which his family was to live. God put the man in the garden and made him totally responsible for it. Adam was to maintain more than just the garden; he was responsible for maintaining the Father's influence in it. Men work hard to provide for their wives and children but often fail to maintain the spiritual atmosphere of their lives. They are prone to provide things but are not equally committed to providing vision. This is where men must lead.

This is why leadership is absolutely necessary. It was Adam's responsibility to keep the garden a safe place. He was responsible to protect his wife. It was his role to protect her from all enemies, from anyone or anything that would harm her or cause her to go astray. God had given Adam instructions. Adam was responsible for giving Eve the instructions he had received from the Lord. But he was also responsible to instruct her in a nurturing environment. Men today have missed this very important point. Fathers have somehow lost sight of this great responsibility. Men can never impart to another generation what they have lost themselves. Young men today think they have fulfilled their responsibilities to their wives by providing a house. But then, even with a house, the relationship falters because they were never taught how to maintain a home.

Adam not only failed to provide leadership and develop a safe environment for his family, but he also missed the enemy. Somehow the enemy found an entrance into his garden. He was responsible for the garden, not just the woman. The man was responsible to provide protection. He was given the task of providing spiritual covering. The woman had become exposed to the enemy on his watch. What a tragedy! Then to make matters worse, he blamed the woman for his failures when confronted by the Lord. Even after the woman had made the mistake of eating the fruit, even though an enemy had been exposed, Adam did not stand his ground. He failed in his last opportunity to provide leadership. Rather than obey the instructions from the Father, he chose to join the woman in her folly. In the face of the enemy, Adam caved to the influence of Eve. God did not miss this mistake. *To Adam He said, "Because you listened to your wife and ate fruit from the tree about which I commanded you, 'You must not eat from it'"* (Genesis 3:17). God confronted the man because he was responsible for the instructions. God told Adam not to eat of the fruit of this particular tree. This was His instruction, His command to him even before Eve ever arrived on the scene. Adam chose to listen to his wife above the Lord's commands. This was his moment to shine. In this crisis he could have been the example of leadership the Father was looking for. More importantly, he could have been the father he was created to be as well as the leader that was so desperately needed at the moment. Unfortunately, he failed at both.

Lives Need Leadership Too

God has given each person life, and each and every life demands leadership. Insight reveals that life is a process. No one is born an adult. Each person is born as a baby, subject to the process but always destined to grow. No one can remain a child. Life demands growth and requires maturity. This is important because maturity is not automatic even though growth has taken place. Maturity represents the spiritual and emotional growth necessary to cover physical development.

Parents face this challenge with their children. They attempt to teach them responsibility with the hope they will become mature enough to make wise decisions concerning their own lives. Oftentimes young people are blessed with physical development but lack the spiritual and emotional maturity needed to manage it. In every phase of life, this cycle is repeated. The teenage years are a threat to parents because their children now seek independence even though they have not defined it. They are exposed to many things without any experience. Left to themselves, they learn by trial and error. This is a very worrisome time for parents who are attempting to provide covering and direction but who also realize errors can have some very costly consequences.

Marriage is another example that can help us understand this revelation. No one goes to school to learn how to be married. There are a few classes offered to give insight into the marriage experience. Of course there are numerous books one can read on the subject. But regardless of the number of books one reads, it cannot adequately prepare one for the reality of marriage. Marriage demands maturity on every front. There must be a spiritual foundation that anchors the relationship so it can survive the storms ahead. There must be an emotional bond that centers the relationship and reminds the couple of the value of their commitment in spite of potential temptations along the way. There must also be a physical maturity requiring the couple to see themselves differently. They are no longer their own separate individuals. Each now belongs to the other, and if the couple does not understand this truth, their lack of maturity may unwittingly erode their relationship. The fact is that marriage, for the most part, is on-the-job training. This reality alone validates the point that lives need leadership too.

Tell Me What's in Me

My spiritual father, Dr. Myles Munroe, said something most profound. He stated: "Leadership is so important, God hid it in a place where it could not be lost. He hid it inside of each of us." Each man must understand there is a leader inside of him. In every boy there is a man. When potential is uncovered, there is no end to the possibilities inside each individual. Think about this. Potentially in every boy there is a father and a family. In perspective, mankind was created to become rulers, those authorized by their Creator to lead. David was born with kingship inside him. David possessed a heart after God. It was inside him. It had been put there by God Himself. In time, God went looking for what He had put in David. The Father was curious to see if David had become what He created him to be. It is hard for most people to see what God has put in them because life has exposed them to so much more, most of which is contrary to His original purpose. As a result, men get confused about the purpose for their existence. If they are not careful, they will ignore God's purpose for their lives and begin living for all the wrong reasons.

David grew up as the youngest in his family. As the baby, there were certain things he could not do. As the baby, there were certain people he could not become. It is possible he was told he would never become a leader. Most likely, he was told he would never become a warrior. It is equally possible he was told he would never become a king. Most often, people end up doing what they have been told they would never do because being told what they cannot do does not resonate with what God has put in them. In similar fashion, many men have been told what they will never be. When boys are told they will never be a man worth anything, their potential has been sabotaged. David's entire family was in agreement that David did not possess the potential to become a king. Remember when Samuel visited the home of Jesse and requested to see all his sons, David was literally forgotten. He was not even viewed as having the potential to become a king. Samuel came to anoint one of Jesse's sons to become a king, but he had been sent to find a shepherd. This might be the reason why each of David's brothers looked the part on the outside. They obviously had the physical attributes of a king. They may have had some battle experience before they had gone off to serve under King Saul. The fact is they possessed all the necessary components for kingship because even Samuel was taken by their individual attributes. However, this did not move God.

Men today place much emphasis on the outward appearance of things. They believe that manhood is about performance. As long as one does what has been defined as manhood, he may be considered a man. But how many fathers lack the heart to nurture and cover their children? How many husbands lack the conviction to cover their wives even if they are wrong? The cry of the prophet Malachi addresses this tragedy when he cries: *See, I will send the prophet Elijah to you before that great and dreadful day of the LORD comes. He will turn the hearts of the parents to their children, and the hearts of the children to their parents; or else I will come and strike the land with total destruction* (Malachi 4:5–6). The problem is not that there are no fathers, but rather that their hearts have been turned away from their created purpose. Men were created to be fathers. This means more than just impregnating a woman. Adam was responsible for Eden. This was the place where his family was to live. He was responsible to keep his household covered and to ensure he represented his heavenly Father's will before them. Fathers must understand that they will be respected by their children when their priority is the preservation of the family, not just the ability to provide gifts for everyone.

Because Adam had somehow become distracted, permitting his wife to be exposed to an enemy while under his covering, this scenario repeated itself in his seed. He obviously was distracted to the point that he failed as well in teaching his sons about the heart of God. Where was Adam's heart toward God when it came to his sons? Cain and Abel apparently knew about working. They were both employed. In similar fashion, they had been to church. Each of them bought their offering to the Lord. But had they been taught about the true nature of sin and its consequences? How much time had Adam, as a father, spent with them teaching them about the fear of the Lord? It may be coincidental, but there is no mention of Adam bringing an offering to God after his fall. Is this to imply that his attitude and his heart were not right toward God? In any case, it is the heavenly Father who shares with Cain the intricacies of sin and its consequences. The heavenly Father discerned something in Cain of which He was not the source. He revealed to Cain that his potential had been tampered with. If he was not careful, he would end up becoming something he was never created to be. Every man must understand fundamentally who he is and what the heavenly Father has put in him. Each man must realize that who he is has always been more important than what he does. If Cain never came to grips with who he was, he was liable to become anything. Ultimately, he killed his own brother. It is understood this was never who he was created to be. He became a murderer. How many men have become something they were never created to be?

David had many opportunities to fall into this same trap. The enemy is intentional about confusing men about their identities. Far too many men today have twisted and warped ideas about what it means to be a man. In contrast, they are less confused about what a man is supposed to do. David was confronted at a young age with the knowledge that he was to become king of Israel. This was a lot for a young man to handle. Had David ever thought of himself as a king? It is not farfetched to believe he considered himself a shepherd. This was his first responsibility. He had been sent to tend the sheep. This was his role. It was while he was in the field that he realized how dependent on him the sheep were. He also became sensitive to their weaknesses and, how predictable they were. His role as shepherd demanded he anticipate their needs and find solutions as their leader. As a shepherd he realized the weight of this responsibility. But probably more important was the time he had alone with the Father. These quiet moments represented opportunities for fellowship with the Lord. It was in those moments that a worshipper was born. It was during those seasons his heart was captured. In the field David had unlimited time with his God. As he prayed, meditated, and worshipped, God revealed to him who He was. David learned these lessons well. The psalms are a fitting testimony to the fact he knew his Shepherd. Men must realize their need for quiet times with the Father. God wants to transform men by their relationship with Him. In the night watch, men can learn the voice of the Father. The breaking of the day is also a perfect time to acknowledge the Lord as the center of one's joy.

If men are to realize what is in them, they must hear it from their Creator. He alone must reveal to every man his purpose. No one else besides Him knows the true identity of each man. In the quiet places of life, the Father shares with every man his potential and responsibility to provide spiritual covering. The lessons he learns in private will become his testimony in public. David learned these lessons well. He knew firsthand the faithfulness of his God. Goliath was no different than the bear or the lion, because David had learned to depend on the Lord. He had already been tested and knew for himself how faithful God was. He worshipped God simply for who He was. He learned to respect His word and to heed His commands. David realized his personal failures were not really personal. A mature man acknowledges his failures while realizing others are always affected by his choices. Each man must be taught that his decisions make lasting impressions on those in his own home. He will make decisions differently in light of this revelation. He will never again make selfish decisions but consider the ramifications on those he loves. Like David, every man must begin with his relationship with his Creator. In spite of his limitations, David was humble before his God.

> *Have mercy on me, O God, according to your unfailing love; according to your great compassion blot out my transgressions. Wash away all my iniquity and cleanse me from my sin. For I know my transgressions, and my sin is always before me. Against you, you only, have I sinned and done what is evil in your sight, so that you are right in your verdict and justified when you judge. Surely I was sinful at birth, sinful from the time my mother conceived me. Yet you desired faithfulness even in the womb; you taught me wisdom in that secret place. Cleanse me with hyssop, and I will be clean; wash me, and I will be whiter than snow. Let me hear joy and gladness; let the bones you have crushed rejoice. Hide your face from my sins and blot out all my iniquity. Create in me a pure heart, O God, and renew a steadfast spirit within me. Do not cast me from your presence or take your Holy Spirit from me. Restore to me the joy of your salvation and grant me a willing spirit, to sustain me. Then I will teach transgressors your ways, and sinners will turn back to you.*
> —Psalm 51:1–13

Hear the heart of David. He was broken before his God, and the fact that he was a king did not change this reality. Not every man can admit his faults; this was certainly the case with King Saul. David was truly convicted by God's Spirit even in his sin. He never became confused about authority. May this humble spirit be found in all men.

Chapter 10

KNOWING WHAT NOT TO TOUCH

Life Can Be Confusing

After Saul returned from pursuing the Philistines, he was told, "David is in the desert of En Gedi." So Saul took three thousand able young men from all Israel and set out to look for David and his men near the Crags of the Wild Goats. He came to the sheep pens along the way; a cave was there, and Saul went in to relieve himself. David and his men were far back in the cave.

—1 SAMUEL 24:1–3

The record shows Saul had returned from pursuing his enemy, the Philistines. In fact, Israel and the Philistines had been at war for some time. Both Saul and David were connected here. David had slain Goliath, the Philistine champion, while Saul had offered him his armor. It would have been a victory both could have shared. David had won the battle with the giant, but it was also a victory for King Saul and all of Israel. If things had been normal, Saul would have appreciated David, elevated him to a position of honor, and ensured that no one would ever forget his contribution to the welfare of his people. However,

Samuel shared something totally contrary to this version of the story. Saul, having been told of the whereabouts of David, took 3,000 men and pursued him. Who is the enemy? It is possible to become confused about who the real enemy is. In fact, people have been known to make enemies out of their own families. Those who are closest somehow find themselves in an awkward position. David found himself on the run from his own people. As opposed to being appreciated for his victories over the Philistines, he found himself being pursued as well. What are people supposed to do when they find themselves as enemies but have done nothing wrong?

King Saul was bent on pursuing David. His motive was not a secret. He wanted David dead; he was a threat to his throne. Everyone was aware of this madness. Those who followed Saul knew he was wrong in his pursuit of David. In similar fashion, those who were with David realized his innocence and were equally confused about their plight as a result of their association with him. After all, King Saul was pursuing them as well. They had joined David on the run. They, too, realized they could not return home until that confusion was dealt with. More than likely they had shared their feelings with David. They had thought many times about what their lives would have been like if they had not had to run and hide all the time. David's men did not hide their feelings. They were sure what they would do, given the right opportunity. However, there was one small problem. They were not leading David, they were following him. Unknown by Saul, he had wandered right into their presence. They could not have planned it better. They were hiding far back in a cave because they feared being caught by King Saul and his men. Who would have ever believed King Saul himself would wander into the same cave?

The men said, "This is the day the LORD spoke of when He said to you, 'I will give your enemy into your hands for you to deal with as you wish.'" Then

David crept up unnoticed and cut off a corner of Saul's robe (1 Samuel 24:4). What was David doing? What was David thinking? Was he confused whether or not this was really King Saul? Obviously he has talked about the day the Lord would avenge him of his enemies. Apparently his men were not confused. They immediately wanted to take advantage of the opportunity. Most men would think that if the Lord delivered your enemy into your very hands, He must mean for that enemy to die! Notice Saul was the enemy of David. He was pursuing him with 3,000 chosen men. David's men saw Saul as the enemy. This moment was a sign to them. They could end their perceived confusion. They would not have to run anymore and would no longer need to hide. But for whatever reason, David did not share in their enthusiasm. He was not as excited as they were about that moment and its potential. In fact David did some-thing that confused them even more. Rather than kill the king while he had a chance, he did not even make his presence known and only cut off a corner of the king's robe. Something was wrong with David. This was not how the story was supposed to end. Then to complicate matters more, David became upset with himself. *Afterward, David was conscience-stricken for having cut off a corner of his robe. He said to his men, "The LORD forbid that I should do such a thing to my master, the LORD's anointed, or lay my hand on him, for he is the anointed of the LORD." With these words David rebuked his men and did not allow them to attack Saul. And Saul left the cave and went his way* (1 Samuel 24:5–7).

There are a number of things implied here. First, some of David's men, if not all of them, wanted to kill King Saul themselves. If David was not going to do it, they would have done it for him. David had to rebuke his own men. This was a most challenging moment for him. Saul was wrong. He was proud and arrogant. He had misrepresented David's reputation among the people of Israel. He also had abused his authority as king by lording it over the men who followed him. No one could deny the king, nor would anyone confront him. He was sick, and when he needed help most, no man confronted him with the truth. Next, David demonstrated a level of spiritual maturity that served as an example to all his men and to every man today. Although David knew Saul was tormented, confused, and just plain wrong in his pursuit of him and his men, he still called him master. In spite of Saul's relentless determination to kill him, he still acknowledged Saul's lordship over his life. This level of maturity is rare among most believers.

David's men are an example of this point. Saul was pursuing them; therefore, he was the enemy. To them he was just another man on the other side of the battlefield. They had forgotten who he really was and what he represented. Even though he was a king gone mad, he still represented God's authority and was ultimately responsible for maintaining God's order in the land. Like the king himself, David's men were just as confused. They had lost their sense of order. They had become blind to their God-ordained responsibility. In the midst of chaos, someone has to lead. In other words, someone must take the responsibility to restore order. David's men missed the opportunity to represent true authority. They were upset with King Saul but had also sunk to his level of pain and suffering. They wanted to take matters into their own hands, and the opportunity to fulfill their twisted motives had apparently arrived.

Unfortunately this is what men are prone to do today. When faced with seemingly insurmountable odds, men, more times than not, take matters into their own hands. They respond in the flesh, failing to represent their heavenly Father. This response often adds to the confusion and rarely results in the restoration of order in their lives or the lives of their families. Like David, men must be committed to restoring order regardless of the challenge before them. If a man's wife and children have lost sight of the will of God, the man must remain focused. If family members themselves have gone mad and now appear as the enemy, it is the man's responsibility to keep all things in perspective. David was under pressure, but he still acknowledged King Saul as his master. He understood that King Saul represented the Lord's anointed, even though he was not acting like one. When men lose sight of their responsibility to maintain the order of God, they expose themselves and their families to the devises of their true enemy, Satan.

David became conscience-stricken. In other words, David found himself under conviction. He first realized his own motives. His men had his ear. He was truly under pressure. He was upset with his situation and rightfully so. He was just as confused about his predicament as anyone else. He had no answer for Saul's intent to kill him. He was on the run without really knowing why. God had brought his enemy to him, and this meant he was supposed to eliminate him. David became aware that his responsibility was bigger than the moment, even bigger than King Saul. David came face-to-face with the Lord and realized He was truly the Master. He could not touch Saul because he could not touch the Lord's anointed. He called Saul master because he finally realized he was the Father's representative of authority. Even if Saul was confused, totally misrepresenting his role and his responsibility, David had to accept his own responsibility to lead. Saul had led the people into chaos. David would not repeat this mistake with his own men. As a result, he rebuked his own men and did not allow them to attack the king. In terms of the family, men sometimes have to rebuke their own wives, even their children. This is absolutely necessary to prevent them from doing something that will only multiply the confusion they are already experiencing. In the midst of this kind of chaos, men must maintain order as their first priority.

Realizing Your Own Anointing

I am writing these things to you about those who are trying to lead you astray. As for you, the anointing you received from Him remains in you, and you do not need anyone to teach you. But as His anointing teaches you about all things and as that anointing is real, not counterfeit—just as it has taught you, remain in Him (1 John 2:26–27). There are many men and women who, though made in the image and likeness of God, fail to realize their dependence on Him. These are men and women, though given dominion to fulfill His purpose in the earth, live independent of His authority. Nothing can exist independent of the living God. John writes in this Epistle concerning those who are committed to leading men and women astray. The enemy does not want men and women to know their leadership capacities. He does not want them to ever experience living in dominion or walking in authority. He must continue to distract them from their true identities while ensuring they never walk together in agreement. He will pay whatever price to blind them to the source of their strength and the origin of their purpose. Most of all, he is committed to their failure to walk in their anointing or to know the Anointed One. John reveals that every individual, every living person, can receive the anointing. The gift of the anointing has been given by the Father through His Son, Jesus Christ. Jesus is the Anointed One and wills to share His anointing with all who will receive it. John testifies that His anointing teaches men about all things. He also confirms that His anointing is real and not counterfeit. But John also shares the need for men and women to remain in Christ in order to grow in the anointing.

The purpose of the anointing is to remove burdens and to destroy yokes (see Isaiah 10:27). This implies that, first, there is an enemy whose sole desire is to enslave men and women. Whether it is bondage to addictions, perversions, or idolatry, it is not the result of coincidence, but a well-thought-out strategy that always has the same result—enslavement of mankind. The enemy realizes sin is real. It is a reality and can be used to enslave men and women. No one is able to overcome his or her limitations alone. If they are to experience victory at all, it will require the anointing.

The Father is aware of man's inability. He has personally attempted to use man to demonstrate His will in the earth. However, the results are always the same. Because of sin, mankind continues to fail this test. Saul, as king of Israel, failed this test. He was unable to obey the Lord's commands because he became big in his own eyes. He was not willing to represent God in the earth in such a way that brought Him glory and credit. Rather, he took things into his own hands. He usurped the Father's will by making his own decisions concerning the Amalekites. He exalted his own will above that of the Lord by choosing to bring Agag, the Amalekite king, back alive. He even demonstrated his own pride and arrogance by sparing what God had commanded him to destroy. He showed his bondage to darkness and deception by advocating his own obedience even in the face of blurring contradictions. He exposed himself as a struggling leader by blaming the people—those he was responsible to lead—for his many failures. If that was not enough, he finally walked boldly in rebellion by leading Israel against one of its own: David. Saul regretted what he was doing many times but was powerless to change. He had lost the anointing. This is the plight of many men. They desire to change, even need to change, but lack the ability to change themselves. Like Israel in bondage in Egypt, even 400 years of praying would not result in their ability to free themselves. This kind of victory requires the anointing. David had been anointed to become king. He would ultimately replace King Saul. But he was ordained to be more than a king; he was anointed to be different. There is a leader and a king in every man, but this fact is only evidenced in how the man leads and rules. He must not lead like everyone else. He must lead according to the will of his heavenly Father and rule according to His ways. This requires the anointing.

Each man must realize his need for the anointing. Each man must know his need for God and possess the humility to trust Him. Every man must realize the value of the anointing is not based upon what he can do in his own strength, but what the Father can do through him by His Spirit. This demands patience because God does not always move just because men want Him to. God teaches men to trust in His Word, not in their own abilities. Abraham took matters into his own hands only to produce a son who was not accepted by the Father as the son of promise. Moses took matters into his own hands and, as a result, missed experiencing the Promised Land. Aaron and Miriam took matters into their own hands by challenging the anointing of Moses and were literally rebuked by God Himself. The anointing is a very serious matter with the Father. The anointing is about empowerment, but it is also about brokenness. There is a price that comes with the anointing. This price involves a total dependence upon God the Father.

Is this why David, in spite of his own moral failure, repented by pleading with God not to take His presence from him? Had he realized that his biggest mistakes in life were not the fact he committed adultery or his conspiracy to have Uriah killed? In contrast, maybe he realized his biggest mistake was taking matters into his own hands. History confirms this decision of David not only affected him personally, but also exposed his seed to confusion and bitter strife. No one would ever doubt David's genuine desire to build God a temple, but because of his short-comings, he was not permitted to do this. However, because David had a heart after God, he thought it no small thing to make preparation for the temple even though he, himself, would not personally build it.

In the larger scheme of things, this was something that had to be done because of who God was. David had a unique understanding of the Father's relationship with Israel. It was imperative that the Lord should have a dwelling place among His chosen people. Israel, as a nation, must be reminded continuously of the need for God's presence among them. God was their king, and He desired to use them to expand His Kingdom in the earth. David, as a warrior, had seen God's faithfulness over and over again. He knew personally it was the Lord who must fight his battles if he was truly to be victorious. He knew that Israel must never forget this lesson. It was the Lord who brought them out of Egypt and fulfilled His every promise by giving them the land of their enemies. If there was a lesson to be learned, this was the lesson. God had spoken to David about His desire to establish His eternal Kingdom in the earth. He revealed that David's seed would always be represented on the throne of this kingdom. David somehow got it. He realized he must not take matters into his own hands again. Saul was not his greatest problem!

What a Difference the Anointing Makes

So David and Abishai went to the army by night, and there was Saul, lying asleep inside the camp with his spear struck in the ground near his head. Abner and the soldiers were lying around him. Abishai said to David, "Today God has delivered your enemy into your hands. Now let me pin him to the ground with one thrust of the spear; I won't strike him twice." But David said to Abishai, "Don't destroy him! Who can lay a hand on the LORD's anointed and be guiltless? As surely as the LORD lives," he said, "the LORD himself will strike him, or his time will come and he will die, or he will go into battle and perish. But the LORD forbid that I should lay a hand on the LORD's anointed. Now get the spear and water jug that are near his head, and let's go."

—1 Samuel 26:7–11

This is perhaps the hardest lesson for men to learn—what not to touch. A man's normal tendency is to think in terms of what should not be touched. Men have been conditioned to think touch can be categorized. In other words, it's okay to touch some things while other things should not be touched. From this perspective, touch can become subjective. The one who is doing the touching determines whether or not what is being touched is appropriate or not. This is not the best way to learn whether one's conclusion was correct or not. These lessons will be learned the hard way. One finds out that he or she should not have touched something because of the consequences. Adam and Eve illustrate this original challenge. They took the responsibility upon themselves to determine if what they touched was appropriate or not. They took the forbidden fruit only to realize later that it was inappropriate on their part. They failed to anticipate the consequences of their actions.

The problem with this scenario is that men and women often overlook the fact that there are some choices they were never given the option to make. In other words, close examination of the context in which Adam and Eve found themselves reveals they were commanded by God not to eat of certain fruit. In total disregard, they took matters into their own hands, believing their decision was the better one. However, there are some decisions men make by which they obtain the fruit, but lose the garden. They got what they chose to touch, but the cost was more than they could pay. Adam and Eve touched the fruit, but it cost them their relationship with their Creator. As a result of their disobedience, they were not only driven from the Garden of Eden, but they also lost relationship with God. They were driven from the Father's presence. They could no longer receive the directions they so desperately needed. Now they must figure out their identities on their own. Adam was not responsible for discerning his own purpose and that of his family. This is a dangerous position for any man to find himself in. Purpose never originates from the created thing but rather comes from the creator of it.

This is a very valuable lesson for men to learn. They can never impart this revelation to their sons if they have not seen the Father's heart themselves. Saul missed it. He never really connected with God's greater purpose. As a result, he got caught up in being king and forgot about the kingdom. As far as he was concerned, everything began and ended with him as king. He became big in his own eyes and then perpetuated his own confusion upon the people of Israel. Was this the reason he pursued David? Saul was all about being king. This unfortunately is the plight of many men today. They are all about being king. They have forgotten the fact that you don't need a king unless you have a kingdom. The absence of fathers in the home remains a glaring testimony to the reality that men have lost sight of the kingdom. God created man and gave him the distinct responsibility of providing covering for his family. This is his place of rulership. This is where he serves as king. But his focus must always be bigger than just his wife and children. He cannot become self-centered, caught up in his title, and ultimately lording authority over those he is called to cover. Rather, as a king, he must provide for their needs but also their development and growth. He must never take matters into his own hands but remain faithful to the calling upon his own life. He must always be mindful of the heart of his heavenly Father, realizing he is God's glory in the earth and this privilege is shared by the woman who is the glory of the man. Together they have the unique privilege of representing the Father's kingdom in the earth. They must realize this was never just about them or the family but always about the kingdom.

What will it take for men to learn this lesson? Who will arrive at this place of maturity to simply wait and trust the Lord? Abraham experienced this firsthand. He took matters into his own hands but later was confronted with the decision to send the child and his mother away. Peter took matters into his own hands by cutting off the ear of one of the Roman soldiers. He also had to endure the crucible of denying Jesus three times, but he then repented and became the rock the Lord promised he would be. Though Saul sought to touch David, David made up his mind not to touch Saul. Saul was the Lord's anointed. David placed Saul in his Master's hand and communicated to Abishai that the matter must be resolved by God alone. Saul's death was in the Lord's hand and would occur according to His timing. In short, this battle was the Lord's. David passed up opportunity after opportunity to kill Saul. He did not take advantage of the chances to bring his own personal struggle to an end. He knew what not to touch.

Knowing What You Are Dealing With

The word *touch* has many meanings. It is not only important to know what not to touch, but also why it should not be touched. Be reminded that touch is one of five senses and can be referred to as a gate. Gates have specific purposes. In the minds of men, gates are installed to provide access: one may enter or one may exit. Gates also can limit access or prohibit departures. Gates can be locked. For instance, the intent is to keep intruders from entering one's property. However, sometimes locked gates can represent obstructions. Though the original intent was to prevent unwanted persons from entering, now welcomed and needed individuals are also prevented access. Regardless of one's intentions, it must be understood that while a gate is open, access is possible. Even one's enemies can take advantage of an open gate. In this context, men must realize touch, as a gate, can provide access to their enemies. This must be understood, because once access is gained, the enemy targets not just the man, but his entire family.

Enemies are strategic in their attacks upon the family. They will observe the man and his family to see if the gate is left open. The enemy will observe the habits of the family—who leaves when, who is left behind, and how long they are gone. Men cannot afford to underestimate their enemies. Every enemy takes notice of any alarm systems the family may have on their property. He studies his mark well, always planning his attack. Men must not take the enemy for granted. The Word of the Lord informs men of the intentions of the enemy. *The thief comes only to steal and kill and destroy* (John 10:10a). In other words, there is no other reason why the enemy comes. His rationale is clear, his objectives have been identified, and his motives exposed. It is imperative that men guard their own gates.

As has been said, touch is one of the enemy's choice tools used against men and their families. Men must realize this is a device of the enemy, often used to gain access to their families. The enemy desires to use touch to destroy the marriage relationship. For example, it is not always the unexpected shock of finding out a spouse has been tempted outside the marriage relationship, but rather the quiet and consistent drain of marital neglect. The husband and wife allow the enemy access in their relationship and become prey, failing to touch one another. In this sense, they have become too busy, too occupied with external obligations while allowing their own relationship to deteriorate. Thus the enemy has been successful in his ambush of the marriage relationship. Young people have been exposed to so much at earlier ages that they have become desensitized to touch and its affects. The enemy has declared all-out war on their lives. He has determined to deceive them to the spiritual value of their gates. As a result, he has exploited their senses using all means available to influence them for his purposes. Through the mediums of music, movies, technology, and philosophy, he has touched an entire generation, desiring to have his way with them. Men, as kings responsible for their families, must awaken to the reality that their role has always been greater than providing things for their children. They must provide protection for them, but the greater challenge is to prepare them spiritually so they will not be taken captive by the enemy. Everyone in the family must be taught about touch so they are able to discern what is of the Lord and what is not.

The first meaning of the word *touch* is practical. It means "to feel or to handle." It involves making close contact with something or with someone. In this sense, there is always the fear of coming into contact with the wrong thing. This is most likely the rationale behind parents demanding that their children not get too close to strangers. This is also a reality for more mature individuals. For example, there are many things adults have gotten too close to or touched with the belief they can handle it. However, far too many men and women alike have awakened to the realization that they miscalculated the price they would have to pay for simply touching something or allowing something to touch them. A second meaning of the word *touch* is "to touch upon." This definition implies something can be transferred as a result of touch. One may touch something that is diseased. The sad consequence of this situation is the transference of the sickness to the one who touched it. When one touches upon something, he or she must literally put his or her hands on it. Men must respect this reality, being careful about what might be transferred to their seed as a result of the decisions they make. Remember, the Bible only speaks to the sins of the fathers and the fact they are visited upon the third and fourth generations of those who hate the Lord. Fathers must choose righteousness; if not for their own sakes, then for the sake of their sons.

A third definition of *touch* is "to fasten to, to kindle or ignite." It can also mean "to cling to or to fasten to." It has been said that sometimes a person will touch something they are not able to let go of. In other words, the thing touched fastens itself to the one who touched it. This is why there are people with addictions in society today. They touched something and were never able to get free from it. As a result, they found themselves out of control. They were no match for the fire that was kindled or the appetite that was ignited. Every person alive knows someone in this predicament. Touch can be a very scary thing if the individual is not aware of the need for parameters. Paul makes the point when he states: *A man does well not to marry. But because there is so much immorality, every man should have his own wife, and every woman should have her own husband* (1 Corinthians 7:1–2, GNT). Paul implies that a person may be in a better situation having never married. However, because the need to touch and to be touched is so great, each man should have his own wife and each woman her own husband. This is an eye-opening statement. Touch uncontrolled, without boundaries or limits, will result in immorality. Is this not the plight of society today? It's as if no one is aware of the consequences associated with touching things or other people. In fact, fathers should teach their children that sex ought not to be discussed outside the context of marriage. Of course, this seems so archaic or out of touch with the modern society in which we are living. This may also have something to do with the reasons why "sexting" or "friends with benefits" is a reality today. Many young people are struggling simply because they don't truly realize what they are dealing with.

In similar fashion, touch can simply be defined as "influence." In this regard, touch cannot be limited only to the physical realm. As mentioned before, touch can be transferred in many different ways. For example, an individual can be touched in the classroom as a result of being inspired intellectually. Another person can be touched emotionally resulting from a loss of a loved one or close friend. Probably most important and often over looked is the fact that one can be touched spiritually. One can be touched morally. For example, a young lady may be pressured by a young man to have sex. She is being touched morally and spiritually because she must decide if this is right or wrong for her. Often both the young man and woman miss the spiritual implications of their decision because they are more consumed with the physical and emotional challenges of the moment. But regardless of their final decision, this still represents a spiritual matter. The Bible reveals: *It is good for a man not to touch a woman* (1 Corinthians 7:1, KJV). A wise man said the same thing differently: *Can a man scoop fire into his lap without his clothes being burned?* (Proverbs 6:27). The point is still the same. Touch is so powerful, it initiates a process all by itself. It is highly possible to end up completely out of control as a result of touch. The temptation is so strong that many men fail to withstand its attraction whether it is physical or spiritual. In short, far too many men are seduced by the pleasures of touch.

Finally, touch is defined in unmistakable terms. It means "to bring down." As said before, there are some things in life a person would have been better off never having touched. Adam and Eve would agree with this statement in hindsight. Looking back, Abraham would probably reconsider the proposition presented to him by his wife. Even David might reconsider his position and the influence it had on him concerning Beersheba. No man can afford to underestimate the influence of touch. Jesus magnified this challenge while discussing adultery. He zeroed in on the real problem. He drew attention to the root of the matter: *"You have heard that it was said, 'You shall not commit adultery.' But I tell you that anyone who looks at a woman lustfully has already committed adultery with her in his heart"* (Matthew 5:27–28). Herein is the root of the predicament. The real difficulty with touch is that it is limitless. In other words, it can have the same effects regardless of where it began. Jesus magnified the source of failure as originating in the heart. Once a man has yielded in his spirit, what he has yielded to can consume him. This validates the fact that the process has already begun. When Eve yielded in her heart to the temptation of Satan, it was only a matter of time until she touched the fruit. In reality, she had touched it in her heart.

Don't Underestimate the Influence of Touch

Men must again be reminded of the unlimited effects of touch. Its power is not easily avoided, and there is much confusion when it comes to discerning touch in the context of needs. The greater problem is always man's inability to distinguish between needs and wants. As a result, the temptation to touch is only magnified. Satan is acutely aware of this weakness and uses every opportunity at his disposal to entrap men. A man's failure is never his alone; a man's failure will always impact others. An example of this truth is found in the Book of Joshua. The children of Israel had continued their pilgrimage from Egypt. Joshua was now their leader, as Moses had died. God had given them a great victory over the city of Jericho. They had set their eyes toward the city of Ai. As was their custom, they sent men from Jericho to Ai to spy out the land. Upon their return their leadership determined that their response would not require the involvement of the entire army. Rather, a smaller force was needed in order to achieve victory. The Lord had given Joshua and the children of Israel a command.

The city and all that is in it are to be devoted to the LORD. Only Rahab the prostitute and all who are with her in her house shall be spared, because she hid the spies we sent. But keep away from the devoted things, so that you will not bring about your own destruction by taking any of them. Otherwise you will make the camp of Israel liable to destruction and bring trouble on it (Joshua 6:17–18). Here men are introduced to the concept of "devoted things." Some things are devoted to the Lord. The Lord Himself determines what is to be set aside as a sacrifice to Him. Whatever is identified as belonging to the Lord is not to be touched by men. In addition, it is revealed that disobedience to the Father's command can result in access by the enemy and destruction for the entire nation. In other words, one man's failure could have ramifications affecting his house and the nation he represents. Obedience must be a man's priority lest he expose his own family to destruction. Fathers must teach their sons about devoted things. In turn, sons must teach their wives and children about what not to touch. The Lord is interested in the hearts of men and desires to discover whose hearts are after His. The Father wants to know which man loves Him enough to honor His request.

History records the outcome of man's failure to honor God. What should have been a guaranteed victory ended up becoming an undeniable defeat.

The LORD said to Joshua, "Stand up! What are you doing down on your face? Israel has sinned; they have violated my covenant, which I commanded them to keep. They have taken some of the devoted things; they have stolen, they have lied, they have put them with their own possessions. That is why the Israelites cannot stand against their enemies; they turn their backs and run because they have been made liable to destruction. I will not be with you anymore unless you destroy whatever among you is devoted to destruction."

—JOSHUA 7:10–12

Joshua was overcome with frustration at the defeat of the Israelites. He could not explain this sudden turnaround of events. A battle that should have been won suddenly went terribly wrong. His men had been routed by the men of Ai. Joshua tore his garments and lay before the Lord. He was unaware that one of his own men had placed the entire nation in peril.

A man touching devoted things is no small thing with God. In fact, the Father is adamant in His position and makes His response clear. He shared with Joshua His unwillingness to be with him any longer. Although He was speaking to Joshua, it was the entire nation of Israel who suffered the consequences. The men of Israel fled from their enemies simply because God removed His covering from them. But the Father did not stop there. He demanded that the matter be addressed immediately. Whoever was responsible for bringing that trouble upon Israel must be exposed. The Lord enlightened Joshua by revealing to him that the guilty party was among him and had brought unacceptable things into the camp. Many men fail to realize that many problems confronting them are the result of touching things that belong only to the Lord. Not only have they touched them, but all too often they have also carried back home the cursed consequences of their actions. They fail to realize their decisions place their families in jeopardy. In the same way Israel suffered defeat because God withdrew His favor from them, men's families will also suffer loss. This stands as a blinding reminder that men are each other's keepers. Men cannot advocate victory while there is yet sin in the camp. Each man must encourage his brother to maintain the standards of the Lord. Men must know they are only as strong as their weakest link.

The Lord pronounced His verdict upon His people. *"Go, consecrate the people. Tell them, 'Consecrate yourselves in preparation for tomorrow; for this is what the LORD, the God of Israel, says: There are devoted things among you, Israel. You cannot stand against your enemies until you remove them'"* (Joshua 7:13). It seems to be a surprise to men when they are not able to stand against the enemies of their day. This was a high price to pay, but even more importantly is the fact that men will pay for their actions with the blood of their families. Achan was discovered as the offender, and he and his whole family were stoned to death. Each father must weigh his decisions in light of his family. God does not tolerate sin in the camp. Every son must be taught the weight of his choices. As a man responsible for a family, he will be held accountable for the suffering he brings on his own. Achan probably never anticipated that his decision would cost the lives of his entire family.

King David also serves as an example of one who made bad choices. Like David, every man finds himself in a questionable situation or a compromising position. Sometimes it is not the man's fault, however, more often than not, the man had something significant to do with his predicament. David was no exception to this rule. *In the spring, at the time when kings go off to war, David sent Joab out with the king's men and the whole Israelite army. They destroyed the Ammonites and besieged Rabbah. But David remained in Jerusalem* (2 Samuel 11:1). It does not appear that David was sick or had been struck with some unexplainable disease. There is no account of an emergency that would prevent him from going to war. However, it is revealed this was the spring season, the time when kings went off to war. In addition, the record shows that David anticipated the need for leadership in his absence. He assigned Joab the role of representing him on the battlefield. Obviously, this was no small war. This must have been a formidable enemy because all of the king's men and the whole army went to battle. But for some reason we are told David remained in Jerusalem. What catastrophe could have occurred that demanded the king's presence at home? What crisis would have dictated the king's decision? Surely his absence would be conspicuous. After all, he was the king. Israel was accustomed to his leading the charge. But most importantly, he was the anointed one favored by God. Many of his men concluded their chances for victory were better when the king was present, but the king had made up his mind to stay home.

> *One evening David got up from his bed and walked around on the roof of the palace. From the roof he saw a woman bathing. The woman was very beautiful, and David sent someone to find out about her. The man said, "She is Bathsheba, the daughter of Eliam and the wife of Uriah the Hittite." Then David sent messengers to get her. She came to him, and he slept with her. (Now she was purifying herself from her monthly uncleanness.) Then she went back home.*
> —2 SAMUEL 11:2–4

This is a puzzling couple of verses. The king should not have been at home. If King David had done what was expected of him, he would have been on the battlefield. There is no other account of King David remaining home during war times. Is it possible this was the only time the king decided to remain at the palace? There is no indication just how long he had been home, but it is revealed that one evening the king was unable to sleep. Many men face times in their lives when they are unable to sleep. The inability to sleep is not the real problem. The greater challenge is what men do when they are unable to sleep. In the bigger scheme of things, there are many options available to men. Some men may use this time to work. Others may find their way to the kitchen. This can also be a time of temptation for many men. It would be wonderful if the man chose to pray. In any case, each man must decide what to do with idle times in his life. Many men are awake long before they decide to get up from their bed. In times like these, men may be preoccupied with their own demons. There is a reason why they are not able to sleep. David was not able to sleep and, as a result, got up from his bed and for some reason went and walked around his roof. There is no indication of whether this was a one-time occurrence or whether this was something he had done on a continual basis. The king passed up all the other options. Furthermore, it is implied he went directly to the roof top.

Experience, some say, is a hard teacher. In similar fashion, the power of touch can be an unrelenting tormentor. Jesus taught that if a man lusts in his heart it is the same as if he has slept with the woman. Is it possible David had been on the roof before? What is the probability that this was not the first night he was unable to sleep? Had he seen this woman bathing naked before? Is this the reason he walked around on the roof? If he had seen her naked before, he knew exactly where he was going. In fact, if this is true at all, he had arrived at the place on the roof before he ever left his bed. He had been touched by his own lust. He could not sleep because he had already gone too far in his own mind. He had yielded already to the fire and then found himself intoxicated by the smoke. David got up from his bed and went directly to his roof, but he didn't stop there.

What is a man supposed to do when he finds himself in a compromising position? As a man reading these pages, does this sound all too familiar? Even if it was the first time David stumbled upon Bathsheba bathing herself, he could have returned to his room and prayed, taken a cold shower, and even repented. Even as king, he was no match for this battle. Although he was a skillful warrior and a renowned strategist, there were few battle plans he could consult under those circumstances. The king fell prey to the moment. After all, she was beautiful. He sent multiple servants to inquire about her identity. His servant returned and not only communicated who she was but also the fact she was married. Should it be assumed that this should have made a difference? Maybe the king didn't realize this was another man's wife. Surely the king should have realized he was about to touch the accursed thing. In spite of all these realities, King David sent for her, and she came to him. Is there any doubt what would happen at this point? Men need to be real and genuine. Sometimes, even as kings, the battle is lost before it is even fought. Kings cannot afford to put themselves in these kinds of predicaments. Not only would this have unbelievable consequences for the king himself, but it would forever affect his family. Just because he was king did not exempt him from these realities. He must be king and keep his focus on the Lord who chose him to shepherd His people Israel. He must remember from where he has come and not forget the faithfulness of his God. Most importantly, he must never forget he is not to touch that which is accursed.

When It Is All Said and Done

It is revealed that David slept with Bathsheba, and then she went back home. In reality, David sent her home. He had touched her; she could not remain in the palace. She had to go back to her own home and now David could go back to bed and sleep. This is such a sad reality, but it happens too many times and far too often. Men touch things and, when they are finished, they simply send the touched thing back home. How did we ever arrive here? What mistakes were made and then repeated that have shifted the mentality of generations of men? Men must be reminded it was not always this way. Fathers must tell their sons this is not the way it's supposed to be. The hearts of fathers must once again be turned to their children. In similar fashion, the hearts of children must be turned to their fathers. If this mentality shift does not take place, everyone will suffer. Women and girls—wives and daughters—will suffer. Sons will suffer most because they will become fathers under the same curse as their natural fathers. Furthermore, the family will suffer because the seed will be subject to destruction as a result of fathers' decisions to touch the accursed thing. Ultimately, society will suffer because what men do affects both families and nations.

King David sent her home and apparently went back to the business of kingship. He assumed he could return to business as usual. Did he assume that those in his own household would forget as well? Had he assumed everyone involved in this mistake would also return to business as usual? Every man is called to be a king. Every king needs to know that others are really affected by how he handles his mistakes. There is always collateral damage, and kings cannot assume those who have been hurt by their mistakes will simply go back to business as usual. They have been touched as well. Their pain and torment will continue long after that night is over. Men must be told the truth. God is a forgiving God, but Mother Nature is not as accommodating. *The woman conceived and sent word to David, saying, "I am pregnant"* (2 Samuel 11:5). These words will touch most men, but it depends on how he defines touch that dictates his response.

David immediately sent word to Joab to send Uriah home. When the results of his actions did not materialize the way he expected, he ultimately took matters into his own hands. His intent was to use Uriah to cover up his sin. Obviously, he had every intention of trying to fix this problem himself. How did the king look in the eyes of his own family and the servants in his palace? He had apparently forgotten that this was really not a secret. When men take matters into their own hands, they only complicate their confusion. When men are intent on covering up their failures, they only stir up the mess they have made. David had touched the accursed thing, and now he was about to go from bad to worse. Where were the men who should have been sharpening David? When the king needed men the most, it appears they were absent.

> In the morning David wrote a letter to Joab and sent it with Uriah. In it he wrote, "Put Uriah out in front where the fight is fiercest. Then withdraw from him so he will be struck down and die." So while Joab had the city under siege, he put Uriah at a place where he knew the strongest defenders were. When the men of the city came out and fought against Joab, some of the men in David's army fell; moreover, Uriah the Hittite died.
>
> —2 Samuel 11:14–17

David had surely taken matters into his own hands. He was blinded by his own infidelity and was determined to hide his mistake at all costs. The lessons he had learned by his experience with Saul now escaped him. Whereas he had been willing to trust the Father to vindicate him concerning King Saul, he was determined to handle this self-made crisis himself. How far will a man go to cover up his faults? How many innocent people must be affected to cover up his crime? Did David realize his reputation with his own leaders might be compromised by his self-serving commands? He had become no better than his predecessor. Saul, as king, had manipulated his men and abused his power. Now David, as king, had repeated the same mistake. He not only had Uriah killed, he sacrificed others as well. These were men for whom he was responsible. These were not just men, they represented families. Their wives and children were at home praying for their safe return. They were kings created by God to provide covering for their households. These men died, not at the hands of their enemies, but at the command of their own king. A king who was supposed to be on the battlefield leading them against an enemy was at home sending a message that would doom them to death. What had they done to deserve this verdict? How would this be explained to their wives and children? One thing is sure from all of this: multitudes would be touched by their loss with no clue about the rest of the story.

Oftentimes men take matters into their own hands with little or no discernment of the collateral damage their decisions will have. What made David a man after God's own heart was not just the fact he was to learn what not to touch, but that he was also to learn the godly way of handling his mistakes. This is important for every man as well. Men may learn what not to touch, but if they fail to learn the lesson of true repentance, they will ultimately fail again. This is an inner battle that must be confronted by each and every man. He must learn to prepare for war while he is not in battle. He must be reminded of those seasons of green pastures and still waters. He must be reminded of the lessons learned there in the presence of the Great Shepherd. He must stop and retrace the steps he learned along the path that leads to righteousness. He must once again meditate on the Word of God, realizing that he cannot escape the valley of the shadow of death. It is at this point he will again be awakened to the faithfulness of his God. *Though I walk through the valley of the shadow of death, I will fear no evil; for You are with me; Your rod and Your staff, they comfort me* (Psalm 23:4, NKJV). He must remind himself of past battles and God's victory. In reality, it was never the result of his abilities, but the fact that his God was always with him. It was the Lord's rod that prevailed against his enemies. It was the staff of the Lord that brought true victory over his foes. David lost sight of this. He was drowning in his own cesspool with no visible way of escaping. He had taken matters into his own hands, touched Bathsheba, murdered Uriah, and sacrificed innocent blood, but he never repented.

Joab sent David a full account of the battle. He instructed the messenger: "When you have finished giving the king this account of the battle, the king's anger may flare up, and he may ask you, 'Why did you get so close to the city to fight? Didn't you know they would shoot arrows from the wall? Who killed Abimelek son of Jerub-Beseth? Didn't a woman drop an upper millstone on him from the wall, so that he died in Thebez? Why did you get so close to the wall?' If he asks you this, then say to him, 'Moreover, your servant Uriah the Hittite is dead.'" The messenger set out, and when he arrived he told David everything Joab had sent him to say. The messenger said to David, "The men overpowered us and came out against us in the open, but we drove them back to the entrance of the city gate. Then the archers shot arrows at your servants from the wall, and some of the king's men died. Moreover, your servant Uriah the Hittite is dead." David told the messenger, "Say this to Joab: 'Don't let this upset you: the sword devours one as well as another. Press the attack against the city and destroy it.' Say this to encourage Joab."

—2 Samuel 11:18–25

All the things said in these conversations did little to confront the things done in secret. David concluded the matter with the declaration that the sword literally is no respecter of persons. In most circumstances this statement would be true. Every man or woman who enters battle does it with the sober realization that the outcome could be death. They, however, are willing to pay this price to defend their own liberties as well as the lives of their own families. In this context David's statement is true. The problem with his statement is that it does not represent the right context. David's statement is merely more cover-up. As king, he had drawn Joab into his conspiracy. He attempted to encourage him as though it would take care of the darker side of that reality. David had become consumed with his own attempt to validate himself. The point, though, is he had failed at being king. A true king must admit to himself his dependency upon his God. No man can hide his sin from the Father. Like Adam, there is no place a man can hide from the presence of the Lord. As surely as a man lives, God will come by his dwelling place and call him by his name.

When Uriah's wife heard that her husband was dead, she mourned for him. After the time of mourning was over, David had her brought to his house, and she became his wife and bore him a son. But the thing David had done displeased the LORD (2 Samuel 11:26–27). This is probably one of the greatest deceptions: men don't know when they have displeased the Lord. It is possible to get so caught up in one's own agenda that one forgets about the Father's plan for his life. David had gotten off track. He was blind to the negative road on which he was traveling. This was the second time he had Bathsheba brought to his house. The first time was a mistake even though it was willful. But this second time was no mistake. David's decision this time was assumed to be the final step necessary to finish the cover-up he had so meticulously orchestrated. It appeared everything was going as planned. No servant in his house would expose him by revealing his hidden secret. Joab had gone along with his command, and life again seemed normal. Finally, David could relax for a moment. Uriah was dead; the time of mourning was over as well. The only logical thing to do now was to bring Bathsheba home. He was happy. Bathsheba was happy. What else mattered? It certainly appeared all was well in the kingdom. Everybody was happy but the Lord. The thing David had done displeased Him.

How many men have taken matters into their own hands, manipulated their circumstances, and then felt safe because in their own eyes things worked out as planned? This definitely represents a sense of false security. Whenever a man manipulates people and abuses his position, even though others may not see what has truly been done, the Lord sees everything. It is amazing how men can seemingly cover every base only to forget about the Lord. God will not allow those in positions of power to abuse those who are weak or poor. God has always been on the side of those who are unable to defend themselves. Regardless of what some men may think, God will show up and fight for the less fortunate. Uriah had done nothing wrong. He did nothing to offend his king. He was only a servant of the kingdom who was zealous to represent his king in battle. He was unaware of what had gone on behind his back. In similar fashion, even though Bathsheba had made her mistakes, she had no clue concerning the true factors contributing to her husband's death. All of this was the scheme of a king. It appears David had become distracted by kingship and had forgotten about what it meant to be a shepherd. He was willing to sacrifice his sheep while neglecting to go after the one that was lost. David had become confused about his purpose. He was focusing on himself when he should have had his eyes on the Lord. He was intent on orchestrating his own plans at the expense of the Father's plan. However, he assumed the Lord would also go back to business as usual. *For your ways are in full view of the LORD, and he examines all your paths* (Proverbs 5:21). The Lord does not just see man's faults. He is aware of the mistakes of men, but the Father has never changed. He is not impressed or moved by the outward or visible appearance. Rather, the Lord looks directly at the heart. It is the Lord who examines every step a man makes. It is obvious David had gotten a little lost. He was going the wrong way in a hurry. Someone had to expose this exploitation of trust for what it really was. Who would that someone be?

> *The LORD sent Nathan to David. When he came to him, he said, "There were two men in a certain town, one rich and the other poor. The rich man had a very large number of sheep and cattle, but the poor man had nothing except one little ewe lamb he had bought. He raised it, and it grew up with him and his children. It shared his food, drank from his cup and even slept in his arms. It was like a daughter to him. Now a traveler came to the rich man, but the rich man refrained from taking one of his own sheep or cattle to prepare a meal for the traveler who had come to him. Instead, he took the ewe lamb that belonged to the poor man and prepared it for the one who had come to him." David burned with anger against the*

man and said to Nathan, "As surely as the LORD lives, the man who did this deserves to die! He must pay for that lamb four times over, because he did such a thing and had no pity."
—2 SAMUEL 12:1–6

David had no clue! It is apparent he was upset, but he didn't see what was coming. He could not believe anyone described as rich would abuse someone poor like this. Surely anyone as blessed as this would have left the poor man and his only lamb alone. David was touched by Nathan's passion as he told his story. This lamb was so precious! This lamb was the sole possession of the poor man. Notice what is being said concerning this lamb. It ate at the poor man's table and even drank from his cup. This lamb even slept in the arms of his master. This lamb is described as a daughter whose significance is more than just figurative. How could the prophet talk like this and the king miss it? David responds in pure rage, totally oblivious to the reality that this conversation is about him. He is bent on being a king but has forgotten he was supposed to be a shepherd. His responsibility was to take care of the sheep. He was to provide for and protect them. Most importantly, he was never to forget about the value of each lamb. He would leave the ninety-nine to ensure that the one lamb missing was found. This was the heart of a shepherd. This was the heart that God saw when He sent Samuel to anoint David as king. The heavenly Father was convinced that the best kings are those with the heart of a shepherd. This kind of king would be committed to the people and remain small in his own eyes. This kind of king would sacrifice his own life for the sheep as opposed to sacrificing the sheep for his own lusts. Where had the shepherd gone?

Is it a coincidence that Nathan communicated this story using the analogy of a shepherd? Is this the reason why King David responded so passionately? Maybe this story did more than spark his sense of justice. Maybe it touched the core of who he really was supposed to be. It reminded David of his true purpose even though he was deceived in the moment. This story revived in David something that had been lost but never stolen. He remembered his days spent in green pastures with his father's sheep. He recounted his days in the presence of the Lord and the lessons he learned from the Great Shepherd. He could not escape his years under King Saul, recalling the words of the Lord who anointed him to serve as king in Israel. *He chose David his servant and took him from the sheep pens; from tending the sheep he brought him to be the shepherd of his people Jacob, of Israel his inheritance. And David shepherded them with integrity of heart; with skillful hands he led them* (Psalm 78:70–72). The heart of God for all kings is that they would shepherd their families with integrity of heart and with skillful hands. These skills must be learned and are best taught by fathers. In order for this to be every man's experience, this lesson is best learned from their Creator. David must once again be reminded of his created purpose. He was a man and shared the responsibility of fatherhood with God. But one cannot assume because he has the potential to be a father that he has the maturity of manhood needed to fulfill the role. David seemed to have forgotten his calling as a shepherd. This happens when men forget the One who called them. God sent Nathan to remind David of who he was meant to be.

> *Then Nathan said to David, "You are the man! This is what the LORD, the God of Israel, says: 'I anointed you king over Israel, and I delivered you from the hand of Saul. I gave your master's house to you and your master's wives into your arms. I gave you all Israel and Judah. And if all this had been too little, I would have given you even more. Why did you despise the Word of the LORD by doing*

what is evil in his eyes? You struck down Uriah the Hittite with the sword and took his wife to be your own. You killed him with the sword of the Ammonites. Now, therefore, the sword will never depart from your house, because you despised me and took the wife of Uriah the Hittite to be your own.'"

—2 SAMUEL 12:7–10

Now everything was revealed. All of the king's secrets have been exposed. David is once again reminded of the Father's plan and confronted for his sins against God. There is no one he can blame. There is nothing he can undo. He has been confronted publicly even though everything he did he thought was done in secret. He is humbled—not because he has been caught—but because he has failed his true Master. He not only took matters into his own hands; he truly despised the Word of the Lord and had done what was evil in His sight. He must now learn the second lesson. He must learn the lesson of true repentance so he would not repeat this mistake in the future. He must not allow himself to be distracted again. God reminded David of his first love. He had touched the heart of God because he was a shepherd first. He could not allow the role of a king to erase this foundational truth. God has always been more impressed with the man as opposed to the title. The Father is never moved by the outward appearance, but still looks to the heart. God wants to know if men have learned these lessons. David's own words speak for him:

Have mercy on me, O God, according to your unfailing love; according to your great compassion blot out my transgressions. Wash away all my iniquity and cleanse me from my sin. For I know my transgressions, and my sin is always before me. Against you, you only, have I sinned and done what is evil in your sight; so you are right in your verdict and justified when you judge. Surely I was sinful at birth, sinful from the time my mother conceived me. Yet you desired faithfulness even in the womb; you taught me wisdom in that secret place. Cleanse me with hyssop, and I will be clean; wash me, and I will be whiter than snow. Let me hear joy and gladness; let the bones you have crushed rejoice. Hide your face from my sins and blot out all my iniquity. Create in me a pure heart, O God, and renew a steadfast spirit within me. Do not cast me from your presence or take your Holy Spirit from me. Restore to me the joy of your salvation and grant me a willing spirit, to sustain me. Then I will teach transgressors your ways, and sinners will turn back to you.

—Psalm 51:1–13

May every man learn this lesson well. When it is all said and done, it is against God that a man sins. May each man learn what not to touch and quickly repent when he takes matters into his own hands. Remember that although there is a king in every man, he mustn't forget about the shepherd!

Reflections

I can only challenge you to learn these lessons well. They have changed my heart, and I am convinced they will change yours as well. I remind you that our heavenly Father has never changed His mind concerning man. Each man represents the glory of God, and as such, he must pursue what it means to be a man in order to experience what it is to reign as a king. Becoming a king in this life is no small feat. But remembering you were created to be a shepherd is a discovery that will not only change your future, but also the future of your marriage and your family.

ABOUT THE AUTHOR

D r. Boyd is the Dean of Spiritual Formation for Oral Roberts University, leading tens of thousands of young men down the path to manhood and into their God-ordained positions and purposes. With over thirty-five years of experience working in higher education, Dr. Boyd has a Doctorate in Ministry and a Masters in Practical Theology.

Dr. Boyd is the President and Founder of Revelations-Revealed Truth Ministries, an evangelistic outreach that targets at-risk inner-city youth with a mentorship program. He and his wife are the founders of Revelations-Revealed Truth Evangelistic Center, a local church in the city of Tulsa, Oklahoma.

Dr. Clarence V. Boyd, Jr. and his wife, Dr. Kim Boyd, who serves as the Dean of Education at Oral Roberts University, are the parents of four children and four grandchildren.